ADVANCED FIGHTER TECHNOLOGY

Bill Sweetman

Airlife
England

Published 1988 by Airlife Publishing Ltd.

ISBN 1 85310 0269 Casebound
1 85310 0382 Paperback

First published in 1987 by Motorbooks International Publishers
& Wholesalers Inc., U.S.A.

Cover illustration courtesy of Lockheed-California.

Printed in England by Livesey Ltd., Shrewsbury.

Airlife Publishing Ltd.

7 St. John's Hill, Shrewsbury, England.

Contents

Chapter 1

The challenge

Secret mailboxes, cover names, strange assassination devices and the other paraphernalia of spy fiction do play some part in the intelligence-gathering operations of the world's major powers. Most information is collected by means that are less exciting, but more efficient.

At a given moment, several satellites equipped with high-resolution cameras are orbiting the earth, storing images as their tracks pass over such targets of interest as the Soviet Union's military flight-test center at Ramenskoye, near Moscow, or the US Air Force's secret test facility at Groom Lake, Nevada. At the same time, an SR-71 Blackbird reconnaissance aircraft sweeps down the East German border at Mach 3, with powerful sensors capable of obtaining useful imagery of subjects more than a hundred miles from its track. Its track crosses that of a slower TR-1 reconnaissance aircraft, orbiting many thousands of feet below and picking up the fragments of electronic signals which inevitably leak across the border. Within the same area, members of a Western military mission—not spies but observers, licensed by international treaty—may be logging movements at a Soviet air base in East Germany.

Information from all these sources floods into a variety of government agencies—even the Soviet Union has never managed to endow a single intelligence agency with a monopoly—which have the job of transforming the data stream into a clear, panoramic picture on which managers and commanders can act.

Intelligence has a peculiar importance to Western defense planning because the assumed adversary, the Soviet Union, has made secrecy part of its national culture. While Western governments keep many secrets, and some have extremely rigorous secrecy laws on their statute books, the Soviet Union is unique in its universal application of "need-to-know" principles. Essentially, no citizen of the Soviet Union is encouraged to know more about what is going on around them than he or she needs to know to function within the system. This principle is visible in the Soviet press as well, where modern Soviet military aircraft are seldom if ever identified in photograph captions. Even in technical textbooks, points are more often illustrated with references to Western aircraft and the Western technical press than by examples of Soviet design.

Intelligence data and an understanding of the Soviet system are blended by Western specialists in the military, industry and government in an effort to project trends in "the threat"—the umbrella term for Soviet hardware, deployment and doctrine. The objective is to tailor the response closely to the threat, so as to counter it effectively without wasting money.

Fortunately, there are at least some parallels between Soviet and Western planning processes. The time taken to bring a new aircraft into large-scale service is considerable, in both cases, and this should reduce the risk of surprise. The laws of aerodynamics and the principles of aircraft design are a constant, and given the approximate size and shape of a prototype aircraft—data that a satellite can acquire accurately—an analyst can guess, with reasonable confidence, what that aircraft will be capable of doing, and what its mission is most likely to be.

Most of the fighter aircraft now in service with the Soviet armed forces (the Soviet Union has no unified air force) are developed from prototypes that first flew in the mid-1960s. It was therefore no surprise when, in 1977 and 1978, Western reconnais-

Unquestionably the progenitor of most of the current generation of combat aircraft, the McDonnell Douglas F-4 Phantom outclassed its contemporaries in every significant measure of performance when it entered service in 1961. This early publicity photo shows the fighter carrying six AIM-7 missiles; no other fighter could carry more than two. Beneath the radome which houses its 36-inch radar antenna is an early infrared search and track (IRST) sensor. As well as capturing almost every speed and altitude record, the F-4 could haul more bombs than any other fighter. This ability to carry heavy loads made it possible to carry a full load of missiles and three large auxiliary fuel tanks at the same time, giving the F-4 outstanding range. (McDonnell Douglas)

The antithesis of the Phantom was the Soviet Union's Mikoyan MiG-21, which in its initial version had little more than one-third as much installed thrust as the US fighter. This is a late-model MiG-21bis, with an internal gun and semi-active radar homing (SARH) AA-2-2 missiles on the outer wing pylons. However, the Soviet Union appears to have abandoned the idea of lightweight fighters. (US Department of Defense)

Smaller than the F-4 but twice the size of the MiG-21, the Mikoyan MiG-23 was developed as a long-range fighter to emulate the radar and weapon capability of the US fighter. The large radome – indicative of a long-range radar – and the IRST sensor beneath the nose are prominent. (US Department of Defense)

This late-model MiG-23, known to NATO as Flogger-G, has a higher takeoff weight than earlier versions and provision for two underwing drop tanks, all in the interests of range. However, the fighter still suffers from poor maneuverability, a lack of cockpit visibility (note the low canopy roof, heavily framed windshield and the position of the inlet ramps) and is vulnerable in combat. (US Department of Defense)

Another good example of Soviet fighter design in the 1960s is the Mikoyan MiG-25. Extremely fast in a straight line, but weak in maneuverability, the MiG-25 is used as an interceptor and reconnaissance aircraft. It was originally assessed as a multirole air-superiority fighter by Western intelligence agencies, causing near-total panic at times. (US Department of Defense)

sance satellites making their routine sweeps over Ramenskoye observed new designs under test, in numbers indicating that intensive prototype testing—the approximate Soviet equivalent of full-scale development—was getting under way.

Three aircraft in particular were assigned temporary designations. RAM-J was distinguished by its wide, unswept wing, and was clearly a subsonic ground-attack aircraft. RAM-K and RAM-L were fighters; the former was a big swing-wing aircraft, the size of the US Navy's F-14, while the latter fell between the US Air Force's F-16 and F-15 in size. Again, none of these developments was too surprising, for reasons going back to the previous generation of Soviet fighters.

The Soviet Union had started planning its prior generation of aircraft in the early 1960s. At that time, the McDonnell F-4B Phantom II dominated the world fighter scene. Far more heavily armed than any contemporary fighter, equipped with the most powerful fighter radar in the world, possessing a very long range and capable of landing on a carrier to boot, the F-4B had dazzled the aviation world by capturing more absolute official records than any other aircraft in history.

The F-4's positive qualities were emulated in the fast, long-legged and heavily armed Mikoyan MiG-23, designed in 1964-65, flown in 1967 and delivered to service units in the early 1970s. But the US fighter's weak points were both reflected and magnified, possibly because the Soviet planning process tends to exclude experienced service pilots. The MiG-23's swing-wing configuration, excellent for payload and range, was extremely poor for maneuverability. With wings swept fully aft, the

First of the current generation of fighters was the Grumman F-14 Tomcat. At the time of its debut, it seemed as bizarre in appearance as the F-4 had appeared a decade earlier. Twin vertical fins and advanced aerodynamics were coupled with a new emphasis on handling and visibility. Note that the cockpit sills are well below the crew's shoulders, in contrast to the MiG-23. (Grumman)

MiG-23 was highly stable— that is, a strong tendency to nose down was balanced by a strong downward push from the tail—and had the turning performance of a freight train.

In theory, a swing-wing aircraft should be able to maneuver with its wings at intermediate sweep; in practice, the only swing-wing that can do so is the Grumman F-14, a second-generation design. The aerodynamics of intermediate sweep are very complex; despite drastic modifications the MiG-23 is very limited in that configuration.

Another major and unfixable fault is the MiG-23's cockpit. Combat experience in Vietnam showed US planners that they had overestimated the capability of their medium-range air-to-air missiles, and that their fighters would continue to get involved in close-range air combats decided by the short-range missile and the gun.

The US aircraft that replaced the F-4, starting in the mid-1970s, were designed to win such actions, in which maneuverability and visibility were essential, but the experience was too late to affect the MiG-23 design. The MiG-23 cockpit is faired closely into the lines of the fuselage, with a long radar nose extending ahead of the windshield. The location and size of the cockpit strictly limit the pilot's view of the outside world. The problem is compounded by the air intakes for the Tumansky engine; their massive ramps block a substantial part of the pilot's rearward, downward and lateral view.

Entering service about two years after the F-14, the McDonnell Douglas F-15A Eagle was about the same size as the F-4, and carried similar weapons. With new materials and advanced F100 engines, however, it was lighter and more powerful. Its Hughes APG-63 radar could guide missiles on to low-flying targets and, like the F-14, it provided a superlative view for the pilot. In late 1986, McDonnell Douglas claimed that Eagles had destroyed 60 other aircraft without loss. (McDonnell Douglas)

Vietnam experience also revived interest in aircraft vulnerability. The fighter's ability to complete its mission or return to base is the product of two probabilities: susceptibility, or the probability that it will be hit, and vulnerability, or the probability that a given hit will destroy the aircraft or, at least, force it to abort its mission.

Vulnerability was largely ignored in the 1950s and early 1960s, on the mistaken assumption that all hits would be missile hits and that every missile hit would destroy the aircraft. More often, it was found, the aircraft was peppered with fragments which might or might not hit something vital.

In the post-Vietnam era, designers used computer models to determine what damage a given hit might cause, and arranged internal components to reduce the chance that a single warhead explosion would start an uncontrollable fire or make the aircraft unflyable. However, this experience came too late for the MiG-23. In the quest for range, its designers had wrapped fuel tanks around the inlet duct, and even around the front half of the engine, ensuring that a hit from any direction on the center fuselage would spray fuel onto the hot metal of the powerplant.

The Soviet Union, however, was irrevocably committed to the MiG-23 by the time the first details of the new US fighters emerged, so the air combat lessons of Vietnam had to be left to the next generation. Meanwhile, the MiG-23 went into production on a massive scale. By 1976, Soviet factories were building more than 500 MiG-23s and MiG-27s—a ground-attack version of the basic design—each year. A series of

The F-15 has proven to be an excellent fighter, but is too expensive for most nations to buy in large numbers. General Dynamics' superlative F-16, the most widely produced of all the modern fighters, has filled the gap by virtue of an adroit balance of costs and capabilities. Originally developed against the wishes of many senior Pentagon managers, the F-16 has been coproduced in Europe and now serves with a dozen air arms. (Westinghouse)

Sukhoi strike fighters, swing-wing derivatives of the 1950s Su-7, was also in production, as were improved developments of the combat-proven MiG-21.

None of these aircraft was complex. All were designed for ease of production—a discipline in which the Soviet Union far surpasses the West—and the rate at which output increased was a shock to Western planners. By the late 1970s, the Soviet Union was building over 1,300 fighters a year, more than the entire North Atlantic Treaty Organization (NATO). And while the newest Western fighters were superior to the Soviet designs, there were few in service and none was really mature as a weapon.

While the picture seemed bleak for the West, the prospects were better the further out one looked. As production of the new Western types increased, and more of them moved out of the training pipeline and into operational units, and as their reliability and availability improved, the balance visibly shifted. This much was obvious to

Last but by no means least of the current generation is the US Navy's dramatically contoured McDonnell Douglas F-18 Hornet. Northrop's design genius, the late Lee Begin, was responsible for the Hornet's lines and its highly effective aerodynamics; however, the US Navy insisted that a prime contractor with Navy fighter experience should modify the design for carrier operations. At the start of its career, the Hornet is the mark against which newer fighters are judged. (McDonnell Douglas)

The first Soviet fighter to emulate the performance of the new-generation Western aircraft, the MiG-29 Fulcrum, entered service in 1985. Visible in this view are the unique auxiliary air inlets above the wing roots which, combined with blocker doors in the main inlets, allow the MiG-29 to operate from gravel runways. (US Department of Defense)

The F-18 can carry current medium-range missiles, unlike the slightly smaller F-16, and its two engines provide an added element of safety for operators such as Australia or Canada, whose missions cover large areas of water or deserted territory. (McDonnell Douglas)

the Soviet Union as well. The new-generation prototypes were necessary as well as predictable.

Gloomy predictions that the new generation would start to enter service in 1981 were dubious two years earlier, and proved ill-founded. It was the latter half of 1983 before one of the new Soviet fighters was issued to a special unit for the intensive operational test and evaluation that is part of the Soviet design process, and it was 1985 before one became operational.

The first of the new arrivals was the Sukhoi Su-25 "Frogfoot" strike aircraft, which was deployed near Kabul, Afghanistan, in early 1982. Sometimes described as an equivalent to the USAF's Fairchild A-10 "Warthog," the Su-25 is smaller, more powerful and considerably faster than the A-10, and is better suited to the task of "battlefield interdiction"– roaming the rear area of the battlefield, attacking reinforcements before they can deploy into action. An improved production version of the Su-25 entered service with the Soviet and Czech air forces in 1985.

Most Western attention, however, was focused on the two new fighters; the quality of their design and the numbers in which they would be deployed would be critical to the balance of tactical air power. Some details began to emerge in 1982. The larger of the two types, RAM-K, was identified as the Sukhoi Su-27, and received the NATO code name *Flanker*. During development, prototypes with variable-sweep

Rakishly elegant, like other recent MiG designs, the MiG-29 is designed to achieve a difficult combination of objectives: high Mach number, transonic and subsonic agility, and a strong radar and missile capability. Compromises have been made: notably, pilot visibility is not as good as it is on the F-18 (compare the canopy sill lines) and the MiG-29's range is not as great as that of the US fighters. The larger air-to-air missiles under the fighter's inboard pylons are known to NATO as AA-10 Alamo; they are at least twice as big as an AIM-7 and, unlike any Western AAM, are two-stage weapons. (via US Department of Defense)

wings and fixed, swept wings had been evaluated, and the fixed-wing version had been selected for production. The smaller fighter, RAM-L, was known to be the Mikoyan MiG-29, and was code-named *Fulcrum*.

Outside circles with access to the intelligence community, knowledge of the two types was sketchy until late 1985, when Soviet television showed brief clips of an Su-27 prototype. In June 1986, six MiG-29s from Kubinka air base near Moscow, returned a courtesy visit with the Karjala Air Regiment of the Finnish Air Force, and were photographed in great detail by military attaches and the Finnish press.

The first observation to be made about the MiG-29 and Su-27 is that they are quite similar in overall shape—not brothers but certainly cousins. Both have twin vertical fins, moderately swept wings and large, leading-edge root extensions (LERXs), all of which tends to improve roll and yaw stability in maneuvering flight. The most striking feature of both aircraft, however, is the fuselage configuration—or, rather, their lack of a normal fuselage. Instead, a forebody above and in front of the wing contains the cockpit, the avionics and some of the fuel, while the engines and inlets are housed in slender, separate nacelles under the wing. Under the skin, in fact, the Su-27 and MiG-29 are twin-boom designs like the vintage Lockheed P-38.

Looking at the new Soviet fighters, it seems likely that the designers were asked to match or exceed the maneuverability of the latest Western fighters, while retaining the MiG-23's speed—the MiG-23 is faster than the General Dynamics F-16 or McDonnell Douglas F-18, for example—and providing space for a powerful radar.

The last requirement may seem relatively minor but in fact is an important parameter in fighter design. The range and accuracy of a radar can be increased in two

A MiG-29 banks away from a camera-carrying NATO aircraft. The smaller missiles are AA-8 Aphids, designed specifically for close-range use, and are carried on integrated pylon/rails to reduce weight and drag. (via US Department of Defense)

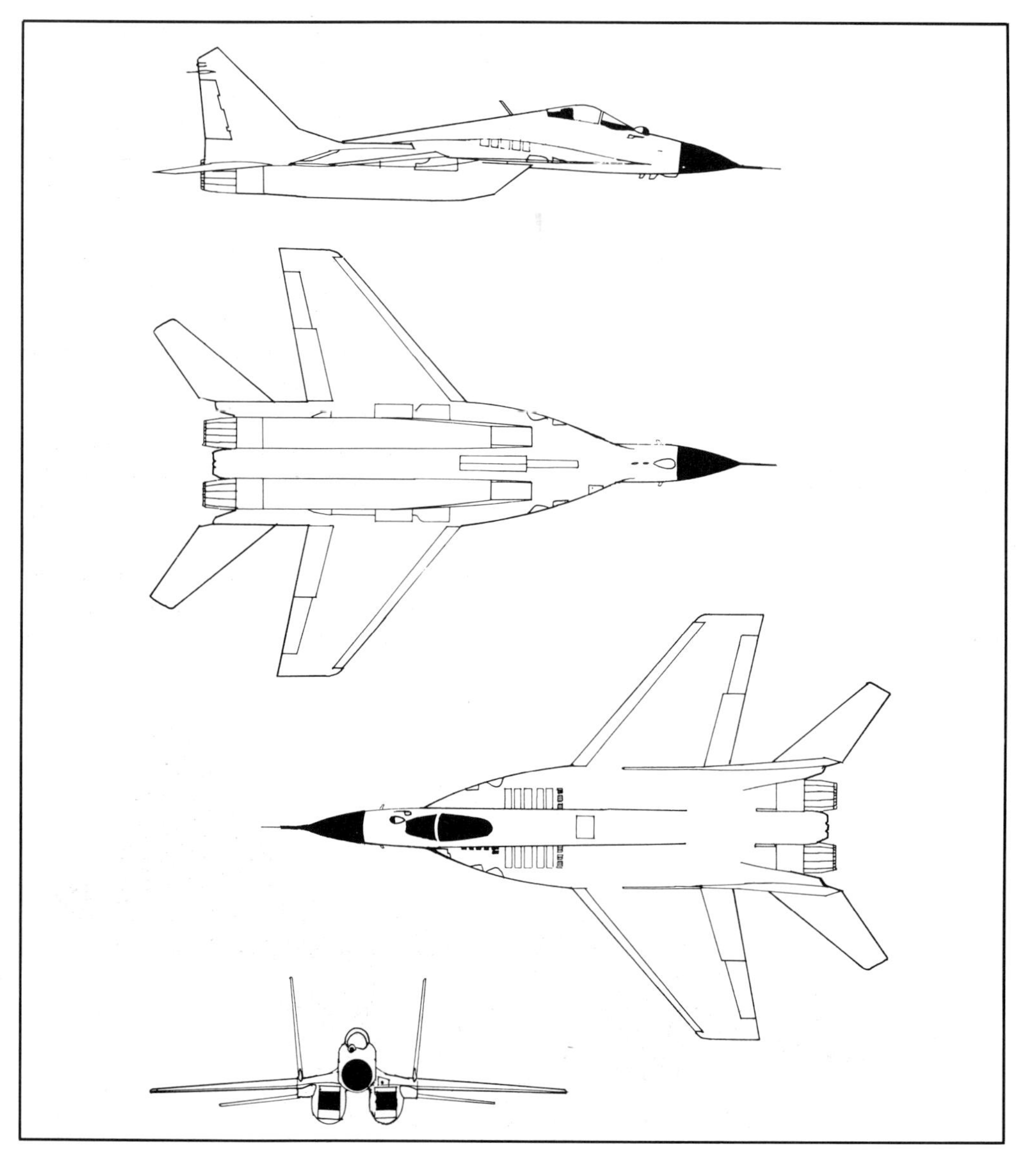

The MiG-29 is not a small aircraft, and is, if anything, rather larger than the F-18. Noteworthy features include the large tail surfaces, set well aft of the wings; compared with the leading-edge root extensions and the size of the wing, the tail geometry has suggested to Western experts that the MiG-29 has a mechanically signaled flight control system, rather than the more modern "fly-by-wire" system. Note, too, the IRST sensor ahead of the cockpit, in a position where its swiveling head can cover virtually the entire field of view available to the pilot.

ways. One is to increase its power and improve the quality of its internal processing, which is expensive. The second, less expensive and simpler way is to increase the size of its antenna. The snag lies in an aerodynamic principle called the Area Rule, which dictates that the cross section of the aircraft should increase smoothly from nose to waist; otherwise, it is likely to suffer a drag increase at supersonic speed. The only way to incorporate a large antenna, and a correspondingly large radome, while complying with the Area Rule, is to have a long forward fuselage. The long, serpentine forebodies of the new Soviet fighters accomplish this well. Both of them have significantly larger radar antennas than do Western fighters of the same size.

Careful compliance with the Area Rule is also apparent in the slenderness of the engine nacelles, which are wrapped closely around the engines and intake ducts. On both aircraft, the main landing gear retracts into the wing rather than the nacelle, complicating the gear but keeping the nacelle slim. Another sign that high speed is important is the fact that both the MiG-29 and the Su-27 feature variable-ramp engine inlets. Plain, fixed inlets are used on the F-16 and F-18, and are adequate for speeds up to Mach 2; however, variable inlets are more efficient from Mach 1.6 upward, and virtually compulsory above Mach 2.

Another advantage of the twin-boom layout is reduced vulnerability. The twin engines are widely separated, so that one hit is unlikely to put both engines out of action, and there is little if any fuel above the engines or the inlet ducts.

Another of the new-generation Soviet fighters is the Sukhoi Su-25 Frogfoot, designed for close air support and ground attack. So far, the type does not appear to have entered service in large numbers, but it is a rugged, readily produced aircraft which fills an important role and frees resources for the new air-to-air fighters. (US Department of Defense)

The Su-27 and MiG-29 differ in aerodynamic detail, however. One Western designer who has examined both aircraft believes that the Su-27 has an electronically signaled "fly-by-wire" (FBW) flight control system (see Chapter 2), but that the MiG-29 does not. Otherwise, the main distinction between the two is size. The MiG-29 appears to weigh the same as the F-18, and roughly two-thirds as much as the Sukhoi Su-27; the latter is about twenty percent heavier than the F-15, when the two aircraft are equipped for a comparable mission.

The way the two aircraft fit into the force has puzzled Western analysts. The relationship does not seem to be anything like that of the F-15 and F-16 in the US Air Force. The F-16 is not only smaller than the F-15, but it has a much more basic radar/missile system and is used for air-to-ground as well as air-to-air missions. The MiG-29,

Even bigger and more costly than the F-15, the Sukhoi Su-27 Flanker is a heavily armed, long-range, extensively equipped air-superiority fighter and interceptor. This prototype was shown on Soviet television in 1985. (US Department of Defense)

The Flanker prototype may have flown as long ago as 1977, but development and production have been slow. Problems with the radar are understood to have delayed deliveries for years; this prototype has no radar. (US Department of Defense)

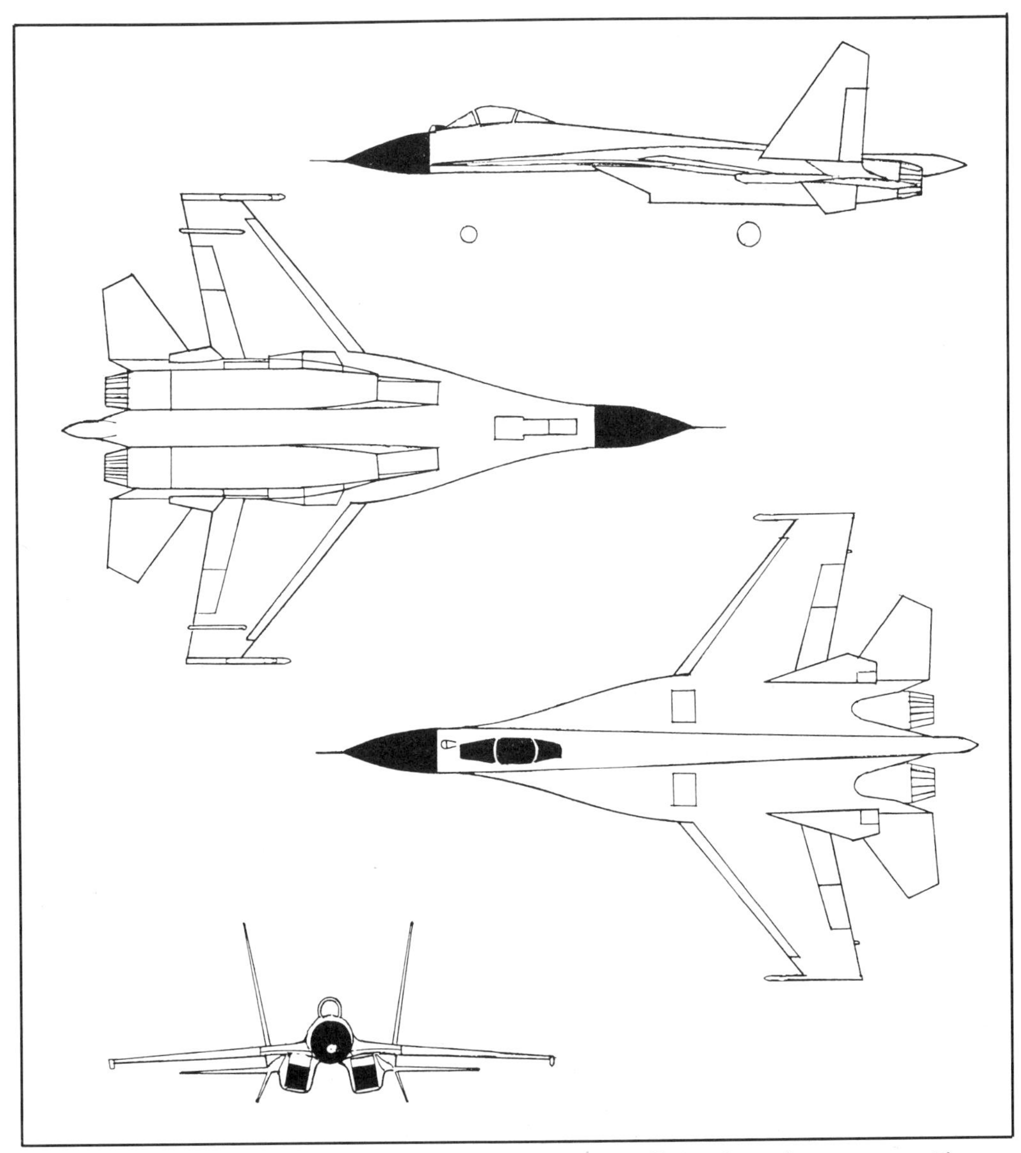

The production Su-27 is quite different from the prototype. The vertical fins have been moved some 20 inches outboard on to new tailbooms, which also carry new ventral fins. The fuselage has been extended rearward into a dorsal spine, which terminates in a tail "sting." Missiles are carried at the wingtips, beneath the wings and under and between the engine nacelles. While the Su-27 is similar in basic configuration to the MiG-29, the shape of the tail surfaces suggests that it is naturally unstable and that it probably has a fly-by-wire control system.

by contrast, has a radar not much less capable than that of the Su-27 (both systems can guide missiles onto low-flying targets, against ground clutter) and uses the same missiles, the short-range AA-11 Archer and medium-range AA-10 Alamo. It also has a rather limited air-to-ground capability because its design provides little space for external stores.

The main distinction between the two seems to be range. Not only is the MiG-29 smaller than the Su-27, it has more power relative to its size and a more slender fuselage. It also has a unique auxiliary inlet system, consisting of cascades above the LERX and blocker doors in the main engine inlet, which is clearly intended to protect the engine from foreign objects which would otherwise be ingested into the very low slung inlet. Together with the low-pressure tires on the landing gear, and the fact that the nosewheel is set well aft (so it does not throw stones into the inlet), this suggests that the type is intended to be used from gravel surfaces. However, the auxiliary inlet occupies so much internal volume—probably equivalent to 1,500 pounds of fuel—that it is hard not to see it as a fix for a design fault that did not emerge until late in the program. In either case, the presence of the auxiliary inlet system tends to drive the estimates of the MiG-29's range downward.

It is likely that the MiG-29 will be used for battlefield air superiority and air defense over friendly territory, tasks previously assigned to the MiG-21. Neither mission calls for much range in Europe. Meanwhile, the Su-27 will be used to break up raids before they reach Soviet-controlled territory, to conduct fighter sweeps over NATO territory and to threaten vital NATO air assets such as E-3 AWACS (airborne warning and control system) aircraft. The advantage of this approach, from the Soviet Union's

Another important new Soviet fighter is the MiG-31 Foxhound. Developed from the MiG-25 Foxbat, it has a radar which is probably related to that of the Su-27, and is armed with the AA-9 Amos missile. Externally at least, the AA-9 is a virtual clone of the AIM-54 Phoenix. Some reports have suggested that the MiG-31 may be used in the reconnaissance role, as a replacement for the MiG-25. (Royal Norwegian Air Force via US Department of Defense)

viewpoint, is that a comparatively inexpensive aircraft can perform most of the required counter-air sorties, including those in the most hostile environment where the highest losses can be expected. Consequently, a smaller number of sophisticated and expensive aircraft can be produced for the demanding long-range missions.

Mention of numbers leads to one of the most controversial subjects in the study of Soviet defense planning: Soviet production capacity. Although the MiG-29 is clearly a less expensive aircraft than the Su-27—whether measured in theoretical money terms or in terms of physical resources—it is still more powerful, more heavily armed and better equipped than the MiG-23, and will cost more to produce. Some 300 of the type were reported to be in service by the end of 1986. The Su-27 is more costly than the MiG-29, and, moreover, has run into trouble; late in 1985, it was reported that dozens of Su-27s, perhaps as many as 100, were in open storage at the Komsomolsk production facility, awaiting delivery of their radars.

Even the US Department of Defense, not always known for volunteering information that might weaken the case for military spending, has conceded that the new Soviet fighters are being built in much smaller numbers than their predecessors. Since 1980, according to the Pentagon, Soviet fighter production has plummeted from 1,300 to 650 per year as older, simpler types are phased out, and, says the Pentagon, "output of newer fighters . . . is not expected to offset production cutbacks."

Soviet fighter production now barely matches that of NATO, France, Sweden, Israel and other producers, let alone China. (Comparisons between Soviet production

Future Western fighters will be expected to intercept and interrogate the Soviet Union's new strategic bomber, the Tupolev Blackjack. Seven of these bombers were reported to be flying in 1987. (US Department of Defense)

and NATO output alone are intentionally misleading; unlike the United States or NATO, the Soviet Union is the sole supplier of military aircraft to the Warsaw Pact and its allies.)

The commissioning of a new aircraft carrier – reportedly to be named Leonid Brezhnev – is expected late in the 1980s, and will add a new dimension to Soviet air power. The type of aircraft to be carried by the new ship has not yet been determined. (US Department of Defense)

By 1990, however, the new aircraft will form a large and increasing proportion of the forces facing NATO and other well-equipped adversaries. These forces have consistently outnumbered the West, for a number of reasons. In the 1960s, the Soviet and Warsaw Pact tactical air forces were mostly equipped with near-obsolete aircraft of very simple design, which had been produced in large numbers since the mid-1950s. However, while Western air forces continued to trade quantity for quality, resulting in a further reduction in numbers in the early 1970s, the Soviet Union adopted less sophisticated aircraft, increased the resources devoted to fighter aircraft, and replaced the older types one-for-one. The "quality gap" between Soviet and Western aircraft became vitally important.

Western analysts mostly agree, however, that the Su-27 and MiG-29 narrow the quality gap between Soviet and Western fighters. Whether they eliminate or reverse it is another matter. Some features of the MiG-29, such as its rather small, restrictive cockpit canopy, are definite disadvantages in a one-on-one engagement with one of the newer Western fighters. Other critical features of the new aircraft, such as the resistance of their radars to jamming, the performance of their missiles and the reliabil-

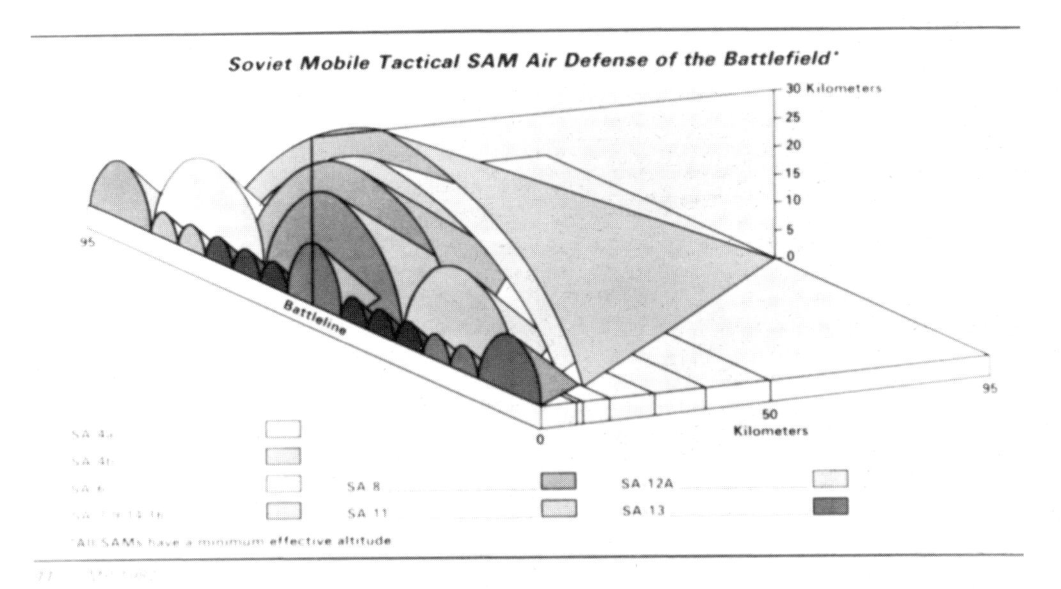

Most Western nations have two or, at the most, three different types of SAM system; the Soviet Union has almost a dozen different types, divided into several classes, along with gun systems. Guns and smaller missiles, such as the SA-13, are mounted on armored vehicles which can keep up with tank formations and can fire on the move. Larger weapons have a greater range and are mobile, but must be emplaced before firing; generally speaking, the longer the range, the less the mobility. (US Department of Defense)

ity of their electronics, are impossible to assess without access to classified intelligence data, and are very hard to quantify even when such information is available.

What is certain, however, is that wars are not decided by marginal differences in aircraft performance. In the air battle itself, individual aircraft performance is important, but it is only one of a number of factors that influence the outcome. At the same time, the air battle is secondary to the ground battle. As more than one USAF general has said: "It's no use shooting down every MiG in the sky if you get back to base and find the lead Soviet tank commander drinking a beer in the officer's mess."

Numbers are a big concern in the air battle. The rough parity that exists between Western and Soviet tactical air forces tends to diminish the closer you get to the front line. Soviet military doctrine emphasizes the importance of having superior numbers at the start of the conflict, and the entire military system—including the design and manufacture of weapons and the organization of military forces—is designed for a rapid start with massive numbers. The Soviet Union keeps more of its people under arms than the West, and billets more troops and bases more weapons on the soil of its allies. Weapon design stresses simplicity, the least expensive way of being assured

The SA-8B Gecko missile system occupies the middle ground among Soviet tactical SAM systems. Mounted on a large, amphibious wheeled vehicle, it is probably the largest practical SAM that can be carried on one vehicle, complete with its acquisition and tracking radars. (US Department of Defense)

the weapon will fire or start when required without any mechanical attention. The system by which the Soviet armed forces maintain their equipment in peacetime is exactly the same as the one they would use in wartime.

Numbers, however, can be outweighed in the air battle. Apart from aircraft and weapon technology, which probably receives more than its fair share of attention, two factors have proven to be important, and possibly decisive, in many of history's air battles.

Pilot skill is one of the most important of these. When the Israeli Defense Force-Air Force (IDF-AF) destroyed eighty-two Soviet-built, Syrian-operated fighters over the Beka'a Valley in June 1982, without losing a single aircraft in air-to-air combat, the IDF was careful to let it be known afterward that the technical superiority of its fight-

Another important class of Soviet missile is represented by the medium-sized SA-6 and its replacement, the SA-11. Effective up to 40,000 feet at 15 miles range, a complete SA-6 system includes launchers and a radar and control vehicle. (US Department of Defense)

ers was only one of the causes of the rout. The Syrian pilots "flew in a way that was very difficult to understand," an Israeli officer told the British magazine *Flight International:* "They behaved as though they knew they were going to be shot down . . . They could have flown the best fighter in the world, but if they flew it the way they were flying, we would have shot them down in exactly the same way." Later, a US analyst who had seen gun-camera films of the combat said that none of the kills he had seen involved aircraft maneuvering at more than 2.5 g.

Many Western analysts blamed the collapse of the Syrian air force on rigid Soviet training and tactics, which left the pilots at a total loss when the battle diverged from the plan. According to one report, the Syrian pilots were trained to fly a figure-eight holding pattern if they lost contact with ground control; the IDF jammed their datalinks, they responded as trained, and were shot down.

The few pilots who have reported openly on their experiences with Soviet fighter training have confirmed these impressions. When foreign air forces buy Soviet air-

The massive long-range SA-5 missile was originally developed to defend the Soviet Union against the Mach 3 B-70 Valkyrie bomber, which the US Air Force planned to deploy in the mid-1960s. It has been developed and improved since then, and in the early 1980s it began to be deployed outside the Soviet Union. Its effective range is around 200 miles, allowing it to cover a wide area from a heavily protected fixed site. (US Department of Defense)

craft, groups of their pilots are trained in the Soviet Union by Soviet air force instructors. Their training is rigid, and set at a very basic level even if the trainees are experienced pilots with combat time. Pilots are taught to stay well inside the aircraft's performance envelope, with ample safety margins. Before a training flight, the instructor demonstrates the required maneuvers with the aid of a model aircraft. At least in the mid-1970s, "hassling," or mock dogfighting, was not part of the syllabus.

Continuing to improve the range and mobility of SAM systems, Soviet designers have adapted a large silo-launched SAM to produce the vehicle-mounted SA-X-12B Giant. Once again, this system must be supported by search radars and resupply vehicles. Each launch vehicle appears to carry its own tracking radar, permitting a battery to engage multiple targets; the tracking radar is mounted on a tall pylon so that the otherwise conspicuous system can fire from a sheltered position. (US Department of Defense)

Now, however, Soviet fighter training is changing. Analysts of Soviet writings believe that deficiencies in tactical training were identified in the late 1970s, and that the Soviet armed forces have made many changes to their doctrine and procedure. Pilots are trained to maneuver their aircraft to their limits. Training has become more realistic, incorporating mock combat with different numbers of aircraft (one-on-one, two-on-two and so on) and against different types of aircraft. Commanders who attempt to meet paper quotas for training missions by constantly repeating the same tactics and the same scenarios are criticized. The need for initiative by individual pilots or squadron commanders is recognized, and the weakness of a system that relies on the authority of ground control or a leader is acknowledged.

Such changes take a long time to implement, and even longer to permeate the mass of a large organization, but the trend is definitely there. It is likely that the pilots assigned to the new and more capable fighters will have had training to match their aircraft, and can be expected to fight more like Westerners than the Soviet pilots of the 1970s or the Soviet-trained pilots of the early 1980s.

An earlier impression of an SA-X-12B system shows two different radar vehicles, a command and control vehicle (rear, center) and a resupply vehicle (foreground, center). (US Department of Defense)

Another critical factor in the Lebanon war was command, control, communications and intelligence, known by the acronym C^3I, and pronounced C-cubed-I. This innocuous buzzphrase actually sums up most of the intangible elements of military operations, without which weapons, troops and supplies are useless. C^3I is knowing what your own forces are doing, making them do what you want them to do and knowing what the enemy is doing. Its inevitable counterpart is C^3I countermeasures (C^3ICM), which consists of disrupting the enemy's C^3I.

Over the Beka'a Valley, the IDF's victory in C^3I and C^3ICM was total. The IDF, unlike the Syrians, possessed airborne early warning and control (AEW&C) aircraft, Grumman E-2C Hawkeyes, which could track Syrian aircraft as soon as they left their runways. Converted Boeing 707 transports, fitted with sensitive electronic receivers, powerful computers and work stations for several skilled operators, monitored Syrian radio traffic and passed information to the Israeli control center. Other aircraft jammed Syrian radio frequencies. The entire operation had been rehearsed months earlier.

Again, though, Soviet-Syrian weaknesses in 1982 should not be read as Soviet weaknesses in the late 1980s. One most important development is the entry into service of the Mainstay, the Soviet Union's equivalent of the USAF/Boeing E-3 airborne warning and control system (AWACS). Like AWACS, the Mainstay is a converted transport aircraft—in this case, an Ilyushin Il-76—fitted with a long-range search radar, information-processing system and several operator stations.

The importance of Mainstay or AWACS is that most ground-based radars can only see as far as the horizon. The curvature of the earth hides low-flying targets; as the distance between the radar and the target increases, so does the distance between the ground and the lowest-flying target the radar can see. From a tactical point of view, the radar's field of view resembles an inverted cone. However, lifting the radar to 35,000 feet solves the problem; the radar can see more than 200 miles away at ground level.

Exactly how well Mainstay works is known only by the Soviet Union, and to some degree by Western intelligence. Like many new Soviet weapons, however, its arrival on the scene has been slower than expected, and it was only just becoming operational in early 1987. Its radar seems to be similar in size to that of the E-3, and it operates at the same wavelength, but that is not the key to building a successful AEW&C system.

Almost any radar is capable of picking up targets at long range; the problem is that the radar is too powerful for the system's own good, and will swamp the operators' screens with clutter unless the system's computers can pull the genuine targets out from the raw returns, establish their tracks and assign an identity to each one. It was this task that defeated the British General Electric Company (not connected with the US company of the same name), which literally spent decades on an AEW&C system but ultimately failed to make it work properly.

Early in 1987, a USAF commander declined to comment directly on Mainstay, but referred to press reports from India; an Indian Air Force delegation had examined a Mainstay and was reported to be less than impressed with its ability to detect targets at low altitude. However, Mainstay exists and is available, and in view of the combat-proven importance of AEW&C, there is little doubt that the Soviet Union will pursue its development until it is operationally useful.

In the other areas of C^3I and C^3ICM, the Soviet Union is even farther ahead of its allies, not because of sophisticated technical hardware but because of a robust philosophy that regards the electromagnetic spectrum as a battlefield. Soviet writers invented the term "radioelectronic combat" (REC) before a similar phrase replaced the more cerebral "electronic warfare" (EW) in the West. REC philosophy was summed up by the creator of the modern Soviet Navy, Admiral Gorshkov, in the maxim: "Kill one-third [of the enemy's electronic emitters], jam one-third, and let the rest collapse by themselves."

This theory unites all REC activities. Military aircraft probe NATO defenses—the Royal Air Force calls it "ringing the fire alarm"—triggering alerts and recording the resulting traffic in messages and radar signals. The Soviet Union operates a variety of converted transports and bombers as electronic listeners and jammers. In wartime, the same data would be used to direct attacks by missiles, artillery and commando groups on electronic installations—which tend to be easily damaged and hard to repair—and to program antiradar missiles. The Western military also has to work on the

Airborne early warning and control (AEW&C) aircraft such as the Grumman E-2C have proven to be invaluable "force multipliers"; one AEW&C aircraft can ensure that more fighters are in the right place at the right time, so that each fighter sortie is several times more effective. Israel has made very effective use of the E-2C. (Grumman)

assumption that virtually every frequency and waveform in the Soviet military would be changed in the first hours of hostilities.

Surface-to-air missiles (SAMs) and antiaircraft artillery (AAA) present another threat to Western air power. The Soviet Union has been far more aggressive than the West in developing, producing and fielding SAM and AAA systems. In particular, the Soviet Union has mass-produced medium-range weapons such as the SA-6 and its improved follow-on, the SA-11, and has designed them so that all components are permanently installed on tracked vehicles. They can keep up with armored formations, to provide protection whenever the formation stops. After an engagement, or after their radars have been used, they can be moved quickly across country before a strike can be aimed at the source of the radar signal. This capability defeated a very sophisticated USAF project, the Precision Location Strike System (PLSS). While the PLSS could pinpoint a hostile radar's position very accurately, the system could easily be twenty kilometers away from that point by the time an airstrike reached it. The PLSS was accordingly canceled in late 1986.

The many SAM and AAA systems used by the Soviet Union and its allies cover the entire range and altitude envelope, from hundreds of feet to hundreds of miles. Short-range weapons include the radar-directed ZSU-23-4, a simple but effective system combining a quadruple 23 mm cannon mount with a tracking radar, and the SA-13, consisting of six infrared missiles and a search/track radar. Both can fire on the move. At the other end of the scale, the Soviet Union and some of its allies use the SA-5, a massive weapon with, according to Department of Defense charts, a 200 mile range. Instead of using mobility for protection, the SA-5 is emplaced in concrete bunkers which, in size, thickness and complexity, rival the V-2 sites of the 1939-45 war.

The best AEW&C aircraft in the world, by a large margin, is the USAF/Boeing E-3 Sentry AWACS. Such aircraft are so important that they are likely to be the focus of future air battles, as each side tries to destroy the other's observation post. (Boeing)

Once again, combat results from the Beka'a Valley should not be taken as a direct indicator of Soviet capabilities and weaknesses. The Syrian systems had been moved into unprepared sites, and were vulnerable; the operators did not move their systems enough and, finally, were completely surprised by the Israeli use of miniature decoys. A massive formation of decoys drew the first barrage from the SAMs, many of which were still being reloaded when the real attack arrived.

The problem in Central Europe is that there are so many SAM and AAA systems in service that they form almost a solid barrier. The classic SAM envelope, or the volume of sky within which it can destroy a target, is shaped like a mushroom, defined by its minimum range and response time at low altitude and its maximum range at high altitude. In some altitude and height bands, there are so many systems that the mushrooms overlap; at lower altitudes, over the battlefield, AAA and light SAMs saturate the airspace. The tactical purpose of SAM and AAA defenses may be served even if the aircraft is not destroyed. The pilot who is fighting for his life against SAMs is too busy to do anything else.

But SAMs are not the only missiles to have a direct bearing on NATO air power. Central Europe is a small place, and a tactical missile such as the Soviet SS-23 can reach any of NATO's German airfields from East Germany. While such missiles are usually regarded as short-range nuclear weapons, they are sufficiently accurate to strike an airfield with a shower of nonnuclear submunitions. These would not be ordinary bombs, but a mixture of mines and special weapons designed to penetrate and destroy concrete structures such as runways and aircraft shelters.

An example of the latter is the British SG357. The weapon descends by parachute, and just before it hits the runway a shaped-charge warhead detonates and punches a hole in the concrete. Then, a second charge at the rear of the munition fires, driving the weapon into the hole. Finally, a third charge goes off, deep beneath the concrete surface. The result of the last, trapped, explosion is not just a crater, but an effect known as "heave"–slabs of broken concrete weighing many tons are lifted out of place and must be moved before the runway can be used. The mines dropped at the same time are intended to complicate the task of repairing the runway.

Larger numbers of antiairfield weapons can be delivered, at greater risk, by aircraft such as the MiG-27 and Su-24. Both of these feature complex navigation and weapon-aiming equipment, and comprehensive electronic countermeasures equipment, and both have enough range to reach NATO bases at low level with a useful payload. The Su-24 is twice the weight of the MiG-27, and as well as having a greater range it is a two-seat aircraft with a large, high-resolution forward-looking radar. This gives it a night, in-weather precision attack capability. The armament of these aircraft includes heavy laser-guided missiles capable of destroying hardened aircraft shelters, and, presumably, dispensers for antiairfield submunitions equivalent to those developed in the West.

NATO commanders can be in no doubt that their airfields would be under heavy attack from aircraft and missiles in any conflict. The response to such a threat is to solve a complex equation involving how many aircraft are available, how rapidly damaged runways can be repaired, and how fast aircraft can be refueled, rearmed and repaired between missions under difficult conditions. Alternatively, it might be better to base more aircraft farther from the front line, outside the range of conventional missiles and MiG-27s, and to accept the fact that the aircraft will have to fly farther before they join the battle. In either case, the aim is to fly as many sorties as possible.

There is one last point that fundamentally affects planning for the air-to-air battle. On the ground, the West is outnumbered and expects to be on the defensive. According to the West's doctrine, the key to resisting an attack is to disrupt the flow of reinforcements, fuel and ammunition to the advancing Warsaw Pact forces, so that they become overextended and vulnerable to counterattack. However, the only means of attacking the so-called second echelon formations behind the front, and the logistic chains farther to the rear, is tactical aviation – strike aircraft such as F-111s and Tornados, and dual-purpose aircraft such as F-16s. These aircraft can accomplish their missions only if NATO can establish temporary control of the air in their target area. It follows that parity in the air battle is not enough. Decisive superiority in the face of numerically larger forces is the goal embodied in the new generation of NATO fighters.

The Sukhoi Su-24 Fencer is a major threat to airfields in NATO's Central Region. It is capable of delivering more than 15,000 pounds of weapons with great accuracy in any weather, and carries extensive electronic monitoring and jamming equipment. (Swedish Air Force via US Department of Defense)

Chapter 2

The Euro-canards

In Farnborough, England, September 1986 was like any other September in an even-numbered year: the streets of this middle-size country town choked with traffic, every hotel between Farnborough and West London block-booked from years back, and the normal quiet shattered by the intestine-shaking growls of fighters in reheat a few hundred feet above the rooftops. On a hill overlooking the main runway of Britain's Royal Aircraft Establishment—a smaller but very competent cousin of the US Air Force's Wright-Patterson Air Force Base (AFB)—the majority of the West's senior aerospace executives, a good proportion of its air force leaders and a slough of others had gathered to enjoy good food and fine wine in comfortable temporary buildings and, between the louder displays, to take the opportunity for some informative and informal conversation.

In retrospect, though, the 1986 Farnborough air show will be seen as a watershed year. For more than a dozen years, with few exceptions, the most spectacular displays had been given by American pilots in US fighters. With their unprecedented thrust/weight ratios, the US "teen-series" fighters could rack around the airfield in unbelievably tight turns, staying right in front of the crowd instead of zooming on and off stage to either side, as earlier fighters had to do. They performed maneuvers in the vertical plane that other aircraft would find hard to imitate in horizontal flight. With only a couple of exceptions—France's experimental Mirage 4000 and, after some development, the Mirage 2000—Europe's aircraft seemed uninspiring. Farnborough in 1986, however, saw the debut of two elegant and agile fighter prototypes, from Britain and France.

The European industry had seemed slow to recover from the shock it suffered in 1975, when the US Department of Defense and General Dynamics beat the European prime contractors—in Britain, France and Sweden—in the contest to supply new fighters to Belgium, Holland, Denmark and Norway. Caught on the wrong foot by the rapid development of the F-16, and with nothing to offer except designs from the 1960s, the Europeans stood little chance.

By the late 1970s, it seemed only a matter of time before at least one more European nation would throw in the towel, buy an American front-line fighter and thereby reduce its industry to the status of a subcontractor on any future fighter program. The fighter market was beginning to warm up again.

The four NATO countries that had bought F-16s in 1975 did so because they

As the Royal Air Force approached decisions on a new fighter in the late 1970s, one factor to consider was the need to replace the Jaguar light bomber. Developed jointly by Britain and France, the Jaguar is an accurate, stable weapons platform at low level, but its ability to maneuver and defend itself against interceptors is limited. (BAe)

Britain, Germany and Italy have collaborated to develop the Panavia Tornado, mainly as an all-weather bomber in the same class as the USAF's F-111 and the Soviet Su-24. The Tornado is considered to be an excellent aircraft, but it took far more time and money to develop than had been planned. (BAe)

An interceptor version of the Tornado has been developed for the Royal Air Force. Four Sky Flash missiles (a British medium-range weapon, based on the AIM-7) are carried in troughs under the fuselage, as on the F-4. (BAe)

needed aircraft earlier than their allies; Danish and Dutch F-104 Starfighters, Norwegian F-5s and Belgian Mirage IIIs would all be near the end of their useful lives by 1980. The other NATO nations, plus France and Sweden, had rather different requirements.

Britain's Royal Air Force (RAF) had bought F-4K/M Phantom II fighters, Jaguar bombers and vertical-takeoff Harriers in the late 1960s and early 1970s, so its front-line fleet was relatively young. The German Luftwaffe had been a late customer for the F-4, and had 250 new fighter and reconnaissance versions of that type. Italy's Aeronautica Militare had late-production F-104S Starfighters, somewhat better equipped than most of the NATO F-104s. Britain, Germany and Italy were committed to the Panavia Tornado, a jointly developed aircraft designed as a low-level, long-range tactical bomber and–in a modified version for the RAF–as an interceptor to destroy bombers and strike aircraft.

The emerging gap in all three air forces was their need for an agile fighter, a need that would become more urgent as the new generation of Soviet fighters entered service. The need was foreseen long in advance; it had to be, because the development of a new combat aircraft, from the identification of a need and a mission to service entry, takes around a dozen years if nothing goes wrong.

The RAF, for example, presented the industry with its first ideas on a replacement for the Harrier and Jaguar in 1969, when the aircraft were brand-new, in the form of

A dilemma facing the Royal Air Force–whether to acquire a short-takeoff, vertical-landing (STOVL) aircraft to replace the Harrier and Jaguar, or whether to build a more agile conventional fighter–was solved by splitting the requirement, and replacing the Harrier GR.3 with the US-developed Harrier II, shown here. (McDonnell Douglas)

Air Staff Target 396 (AST 396). The revival of the agile fighter was still in the future, so AST 396 stressed the importance of ground attack. The aircraft was to be an ultra-short takeoff type, like the Harrier, but supersonic and capable of operating in all weather. However, it quickly became apparent that such an aircraft would be much too expensive to be risked against front-line ground targets, so AST 396 was rewritten to eliminate the vertical-takeoff requirement. Not surprisingly, the British designers responded with aircraft very similar to the Tornado.

Some lean years followed for the RAF, as the first surge in energy prices and the consequent recession forced cutbacks in government spending, and caused planning to be deferred. Between 1974 and 1976, some rethinking took place. The advent of new counterairfield weapons renewed interest in short or vertical takeoff, and the use of SAMs in the 1973 Arab-Israeli war, mainly by Egypt, had a great influence, but not in the most obvious way. With full access to combat reports, the RAF could see that the initial, spectacular success of the SAMs had been reversed within days by Israeli tactics and improved electronic jamming technology. Future fighters would be better equipped with jammers, decoys and defensive antiradar missiles.

The RAF took its thinking one stage further: If the Soviets could no longer rely on their SAMs to protect their troops from NATO aircraft, they would increase their em-

Approaching the requirement for a new fighter, British and German designers had to persuade planners that they could do better than the F-18, at a comparable cost. The radical aerodynamics, sophisticated digital flight control system and comprehensive equipment of the F-18 have made this a challenging task. (McDonnell Douglas)

phasis on agile fighters, capable of engaging low-level, high-speed targets over the battlefield.

In 1976, the RAF issued AST 403, which called for what was essentially a supersonic agile fighter with the ability to deliver air-to-ground weapons in clear weather. It could also be considered a ground-attack aircraft, with the ability to defend itself against high-performance fighters.

AST 403 was made feasible by the realization that an air-to-air fighter could do a respectable job in the ground-attack mission. In the 1960s, fighters such as the F-4 and Mirage III proved slow and clumsy when laden with bombs and extra fuel tanks, and lacked any means of delivering weapons accurately except from a dangerous dive attack. As a result, specialized strike aircraft like the Jaguar, with its high wing loading and sophisticated navigation and attack electronics, were developed.

However, it was soon recognized that the F-16 was different: With its oversize engine, it could maintain an adequate speed with a heavy load (by virtue of sheer thrust), and its combination of precise flight controls, digital weapon-aiming computer and head-up display enabled it to deliver weapons far more accurately than an F-4. In one respect, a heavy weapon load actually improved its handling at low level: With more weight being carried by each square foot of its wing, it was less susceptible to gusts and windshears at low level.

British Aerospace, (BAe), formed in 1977 by the combination and nationalization of British Aircraft Corporation (BAC) and Hawker Siddeley Aviation, has two separate fighter design organizations. The former Hawker team, at Kingston in Surrey, is responsible for the VTOL (vertical takeoff/landing) Harrier and the Hawk trainer; the

For the export market, Northrop proposed the F/A-18L, minus the basic aircraft's heavy carrier-type landing gear and wing-folding, and with a fully instrumented rear cockpit and a system using wing spoilers and the tail surfaces to provide a smooth ride at high speed and low altitude. In the absence of a big customer ready to commit, however, the export sales went to the standard F-18A. (Northrop)

design office at Warton, Lancashire, formerly part of BAC, leads Britain's share of the Tornado program.

The two most promising designs submitted to meet AST 403 reflected this background. From Kingston came a short-takeoff/vertical-landing (STOVL) design based on the Harrier concept, with a single engine exhausting through four swiveling nozzles, but with a form of afterburning—called plenum-chamber burning—on the front pair of nozzles. (The term STOVL describes the way the Harrier normally operates in service, with a very short takeoff run and a vertical landing.) Warton produced a more conventional twin-engined fighter, in a study named P.96, with a swept wing, aft stabilizer and large leading-edge root extension (LERX) surfaces to improve maneuverability.

The RAF saw merits in both proposals. The conventional design was faster, and more maneuverable at supersonic speed, and because it did not need such features as swiveling exhaust nozzles and a "puffer-jet" control system for flight at zero airspeed, it had a longer range. On the other hand, it still needed a significant runway. The STOVL design was slower, had less range and would not be as agile, but it needed only a few hundred feet of straight and level ground for takeoff and could land on any hard pad. It could be based off the airfield, and supported by trucks and helicopters, or it could remain in hardened and concealed shelters on the airfield and continue to fly from taxiways, roadways or anything else that was available.

There was also a political factor involved. It was most unlikely that the RAF, with a need for about 200 aircraft, would be able to persuade any British government to launch an all-British program to develop a new fighter. Collaborative programs, in which several countries pooled their requirements, shared the cost of developing and tooling for production, and then coproduced the aircraft, were considered more attractive. Up-front costs were lower for each country, and production costs were also lower because of the larger number of aircraft.

But there were some drawbacks. Collaborative programs, overall, took longer to complete and cost more to run than one-country efforts. Complicating factors included the need to reach consensus agreements on every change in the program, and the difficulty of dealing with different languages and different codes of business law. Another problem was that collaboration meant accepting a partner's design leadership in some areas, leading to a loss of national technical capability, and could even mean accepting the majority's decision to import a subsystem from a third-party supplier. The selection of a Texas Instruments attack radar for the Tornado, at Germany's insistence, had drawn outraged but ineffective responses from Britain's avionics industry.

For the RAF, though, a most important advantage was that collaborative programs were almost impossible to cancel once started. If one country pulled out of a collaborative program, its partners could well sue it for its entire share of the development cost. This last fact had probably saved Tornado from the ax in the mid-1970s.

Collaboration, therefore, was the only way the British would go. During the 1960s, however, the Federal German government and Germany's renascent aircraft industry had invested heavily in VTOL technology, believing that most future military aircraft and many civil aircraft would be runway-free. Not one of the German VTOL types went into production, and the German aerospace industry and the Luftwaffe were left with a deep aversion to VTOL. France had gone through a similar experience. Arguing that the French and Germans had pursued overcomplicated solutions to VTOL, as the Harrier community privately believed, only made matters worse. In short, collaborative STOVL or VTOL with Germany or France was, as even the Harrier people acknowledge, a nonstarter.

Given the different merits of the two designs submitted to AST 403, and the political environment, the British decided the time was not ripe to replace the Harrier and Jaguar with a single aircraft. In early 1979 the requirement was split; the RAF issued Air Staff Requirement 409 (an ASR is firmer than an AST) for an improved version of the Harrier, and AST 403 continued with emphasis on supersonic speed, agility, air-to-air performance and collaborative development.

Tail-first or canard configurations are nothing new. The Lockheed L-133 was proposed to the US Army Air Force in 1940, and would have been powered by a jet engine invented by Nathan Price of Lockheed. The project was overtaken by the needs of war production and the rapid development of jet engines in Britain. (Lockheed)

One look at the ejection seat shows that the JAS 39 Gripen is a tiny fighter by modern standards. Consider that the F-18 evolved from a "lightweight fighter" design, and that the Gripen gets by with one of the F-18's two engines. The canard layout, fly-by-wire and advanced materials are the keys to the Gripen's quart-in-a-pint-pot capability. (Saab)

The first canard of any type to enter production was the Saab 37 Viggen short-takeoff-and-landing (STOL) fighter. At low speeds, the Viggen's canard not only provides lift but trails a vortex which stabilizes the airflow over the main wing. This is the JA37 interceptor version of the Viggen, the first non-US fighter to have a radar/missile system good enough to "look down and shoot down" – that is, to detect and engage targets at much lower altitudes. (Saab)

The McDonnell Douglas/BAe AV-8B Harrier II was selected for ASR 409, but the AST 403 continued to face problems. One was that the new Conservative government of Margaret Thatcher, elected in March 1979, was determined to modernize the British nuclear deterrent and—it soon emerged—preferred the most expensive option available, the US Navy/Lockheed D5 submarine-launched ballistic missile, popularly known as Trident II. The D5 and the submarines needed to launch it would be the next major British military equipment purchase after Tornado, and money for new fighters would be short. Therefore, in June 1981, the British Ministry of Defense announced that the direct replacement of Jaguar would be deferred, and that Tornados and improved Harriers would take over the Jaguar force's missions as its aircraft were retired. In one sense, though, the outwardly disappointing decision provided a useful breathing space for the British aircraft industry.

Late in 1978, McDonnell Douglas, Northrop and the US Navy rolled out the first example of the F-18 Hornet. The F-18 was based on Northrop's YF-17—itself based on the pioneering P530 Cobra design study—and combined many of the most advanced technologies available at the time. Northrop's fighter genius, the late Lee Begin, was responsible for its radical shape, with long, carefully configured LERX surfaces and twin, forward-set fins. A complex fly-by-wire system from General Electric (GE) not only made the aircraft flyable, but also made it highly resistant to loss of control; even if abused, the aircraft would not depart from controlled flight.

Likewise, GE's F404 engines were electronically managed, and quickly proved far easier to handle than the temperamental F100 which GE's rival, Pratt & Whitney, had developed for the F-16 and F-15. McDonnell Douglas—which was prime contractor on the program, because the Navy insisted that the prime should have experience

Israel Aircraft Industries (IAI) developed its fighter-design skills by copying the Dassault Mirage after France refused to deliver 50 Mirages ordered by Israel. Instead of the original Atar engine, the Israeli aircraft was redesigned to use a General Electric J79. The modified fighter, called Kfir, was unveiled in 1975. (IAI)

with carrier-based aircraft—added two main features to the design: lightweight composite materials, used for the wing skins and most of the access panels, and a remarkable new cockpit layout which enabled the F-18 pilot to control the F-18, its sophisticated radar and many weapons with a small, relatively uncluttered instrument panel.

From the original Kfir, IAI developed the Kfir-C2, with small fixed canards and "dog-tooth" notches on the leading edge. The objective was to stabilize the vortex flow over the main wing at high angles of attack, providing more lift and less drag, and considerably improving the fighter's maneuverability. (IAI)

Fundamentally quite similar to the Gripen, the IAI Lavi is somewhat larger and more powerful. It is primarily designed as a ground attack aircraft, but one which is capable of defending itself against such fighters as the MiG-29, which has already been delivered to Syria. Although the Lavi is basically a single-seat aircraft, the first two examples are two-seaters, so that the back seat can be used for fight-test instruments. (IAI)

Although McDonnell Douglas led the F-18 program for the US Navy, Northrop retained the rights to sell a version of the aircraft for export, and was offering such a variant, designated F-18L (L for land-based), by 1979. The F-18 was already emerging as a very capable aircraft, but the L would be at least 2,650 pounds lighter, thanks to the elimination of wing-folding, a simpler landing gear and the removal of the structural beef which the F-18A needed to withstand the controlled crash of a carrier landing. With enlarged and modified flaps and spoilers, the F-18L would also have been able to operate from reasonably short runways.

The ultimate Kfir-C7 featured improved nav-attack avionics and a new store-management system, controlled by the multifunction display on the lower left-hand side of the panel. (IAI)

Although the F-18L was never built, except as a mock-up, it became the baseline against which any new British designs, or other European proposals, had to be judged. If Europe could not do something significantly better than the F-18L, there was simply no point in spending money on a brand-new aircraft. Recognizing this, the RAF and British industry set their sights to a slightly greater distance, accepting a later entry-into-service date but planning to incorporate newer technology which had not been available for the F-18.

The same technological developments, and the common need to develop an aircraft with a useful performance margin over the F-18, equally affected planning outside the United Kingdom. The biggest single manufacturer of fighters outside the Soviet Union, the United States and China—France's Dassault-Breguet—had likewise been forced to live with defeat after the four NATO nations placed their massive F-16 order in 1975. In the same year, the French air force, the Armee de l'Air, scrapped plans for Dassault's ACF (Avion de Combat Futur), a big twin-jet fighter in the F-15 class. In December, however, the Armee de l'Air announced that it had selected a new, smaller design from Dassault, the Mirage 2000, to perform the air-superiority and interception missions in the 1980s.

The Mirage 2000 is not quite like any of its contemporaries. Although it is about the same size as the F-16, it has the same basic layout as the classic Mirage III, with a plain sixty-degree delta wing and no horizontal stabilizer, and despite much new technology it does not match the US fighter's agility at speeds just below Mach 1; nor does it offer the same panoramic view from the cockpit. The missions of the two aircraft are rather different. The Mirage 2000 is mainly designed as an interceptor, with an emphasis on high speed and rapid climb to engage targets such as Backfire bombers and MiG-25s, is faster than the F-16 and carries more capable missiles.

The first Lavi in low-speed flight. Note the rather drastic upward deflection of the foreplanes; without the computers and sensors which adjust the controls many times every second, the airplane would simply flip over on its back in such a configuration. (IAI)

The Mirage 2000 became operational in July 1984. Its significance to French planning for a future combat aircraft is twofold. First, while it has been relatively successful on the export market, it has not gained as large a share of the market as previous Mirage designs, due to competition from the F-16 and F-18. Second, as an interceptor and air-superiority fighter, its existence has skewed France's future requirements toward a ground-attack aircraft which can economically be used to replace the Jaguar in the French air force, and the Aeronavale's carrier-based Super Etendards.

German plans for an F-4 replacement began to firm up in the late 1970s, under the designation TKF 90 (Tactisches Kampfflugzeug 1990). Messerschmitt-Bolkow-Blohm (MBB), Germany's partner on the Tornado program, produced a number of advanced design studies, emphasizing high speed, heavy armament and agility packed into a relatively small aircraft. Italy's industry and air force planners produced a similar requirement.

Once again, politics became a critical factor. The three key players were France, Germany and Britain, each needing a large number of aircraft and possessing the financial and industrial resources to make a major contribution to the development costs. Dassault, MBB and BAe started discussions for a new European Combat Aircraft (ECA) in 1979, but by the time the joint technical studies were complete, in 1981, the British requirement had been deferred, and cost overruns on the Tornado program had forced Germany to postpone TKF 90. That was the end of the line for ECA.

The companies continued design studies, but both Dassault and BAe had reason to worry about the continued work on advanced fighters in the United States, lead-

The Lavi has a chin inlet, like the F-16. The main advantages of such an inlet are that the airflow into the engine is relatively unaffected by the attitude of the aircraft, particularly in sideslip which is encountered during high-angle-of-attack maneuvering. Twin ventral fins provide added stability at high speeds, in tight maneuvers and with large external loads. (IAI)

ing to further growth in the already large transatlantic technology gap. With no firm air force requirements in sight by late 1982, the long-term situation began to look worse. Both BAe and Dassault, in parallel but separately, approached their respective governments with proposals to build prototype aircraft, largely with private funding, to demonstrate their new fighter concepts. Dassault's decision to go ahead with a

The Lavi's carbon-fiber wing is produced by Grumman in Long Island, New York. Mechanical fasteners are used to secure the skins to the ribs and spars; while composite skins can be bonded together, it is necessary to make at least one skin removable in case of problems with internal parts. (IAI)

prototype, initially named ACX (Avion de Combat Experimental), but later named Rafale (squall), was announced in early 1983. In May, just before the Paris Air Show, the British government issued a contract to BAe for an Experimental Aircraft Prototype (EAP). Then, in December, the air forces of five nations—Britain, France, Germany, Italy and Spain— agreed on an outline requirement for a Future European Fighter Aircraft (FEFA), in the same broad category as the two prototypes. France, Britain and Germany wanted 200 aircraft each, with 100 each for the other two partners. Those unversed in the intricacies of European aerospace politics might have been forgiven for assuming that the program was under way.

International discussions over FEFA—later known simply as EFA—soon reached an impasse. Dassault and the French air force wanted to build an aircraft with an empty weight of no more than 18,740 pounds (8.5 metric tons); Germany and Britain, however, were prepared to go to 23,150 pounds (10.5 metric tons) if necessary, in order to accommodate the radar and missile armament they deemed necessary while maintaining range and maneuverability.

This special rig, using a Lavi cockpit mockup, was designed to test the fighter's air-conditioning system. A battery of heat lamps simulates the desert sun. (IAI)

Not only would the bigger aircraft tend to be more expensive, but it would also require a new engine (the smaller aircraft desired by the French could use France's own SNECMA M88), and another billion dollars or so in development cost. A less expensive aircraft, Dassault argued, would also be more attractive on the export market. However, the other main parties stood their ground, and in 1985 France withdrew from the program.

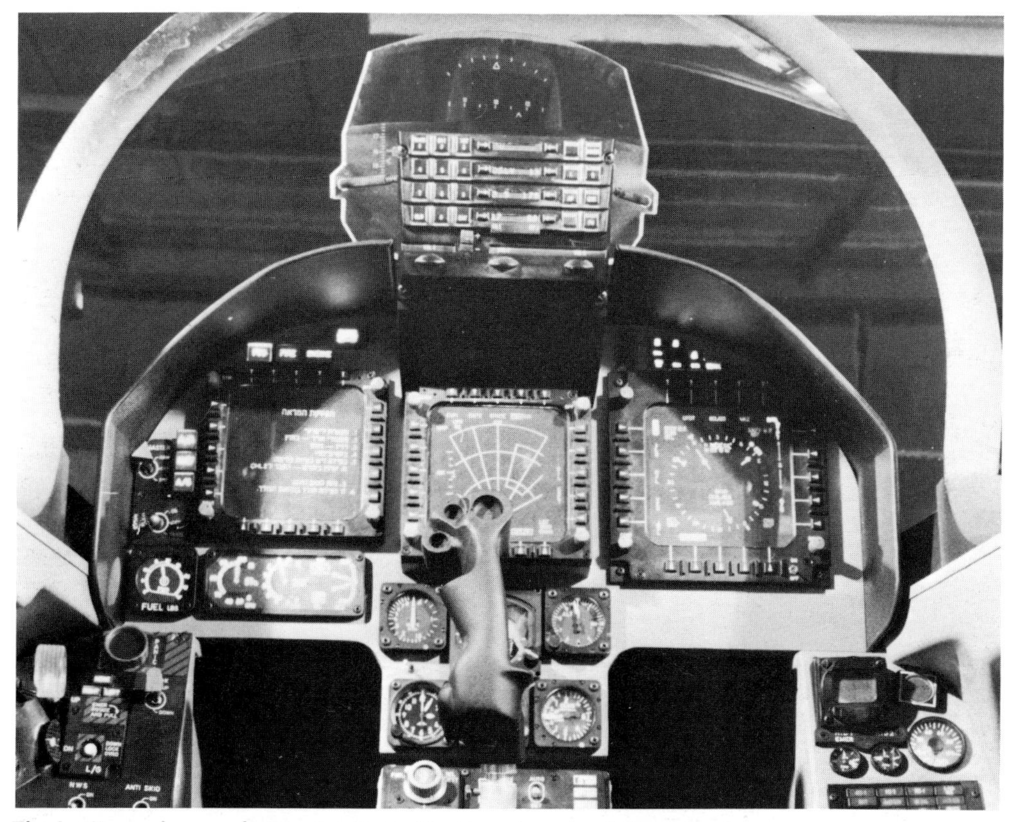

The Lavi's modern cockpit is dominated by three large multifunction display (MFD) screens. Note, on the right-hand display, that the functions of the pushbuttons that surround the screen are identified on the screen itself. If the pilot selects a different screen, the functions of the buttons and the legends will change. The 20 buttons on each MFD can therefore replace a far larger number of special-purpose switches. The wide-angle head-up display, distinctly wider than that of the Kfir, is also noteworthy. Despite its considerable promise, the future of the Lavi was in considerable doubt at the time of writing. The costs of development have increased far beyond the original estimates, to the point where the Lavi program threatens to deprive other elements of the Israeli armed forces of their budgets. (IAI)

In early 1986, as both prototypes neared completion, the four remaining members of the EFA project formed Eurofighter GMbH, a multinational joint venture, to manage the program. Meanwhile, Dassault and the French government announced that the Dassault prototype, the Rafale A, would be followed by a lighter, smaller production aircraft, Rafale B. The first of these new aircraft to fly, on July 4, 1986, was the Dassault Rafale A. The British Aerospace EAP followed on August 8. Both aircraft went supersonic on their first flights, and were the focus of attention at the Farnborough show in September.

While the EFA partners were embroiled in politics and budget-trimming, however, two relatively tiny nations were demolishing the principle that supposedly made collaboration and its headaches necessary. The British government had maintained since the 1960s that the nation could not afford to develop a major combat aircraft on its own. The example of Sweden, which consistently manages to do so, but has roughly one-seventh of Britain's or Germany's population, is usually ignored or treated as a freak of nature.

Also generally ignored is the answer to the following questions. Which was the first Western European country to field a swept-wing jet fighter? An all-weather, swept-wing fighter? A properly integrated all-weather supersonic interceptor? A pulse-Doppler fighter radar? The answer in each case is Sweden.

There is no real secret to Sweden's performance. A long-standing partnership exists between government and industry, supported by a national consensus that Sweden should maintain self-sufficiency in arms to sustain its neutrality. Although the Swedish aerospace companies monopolize their domestic markets, they are left in

Dassault's Mirage 2000 has been the only serious challenger to the F-16 and F-18 in most export markets. Very similar to the older Mirage III at a distance, the 2000 has a fly-by-wire system and leading-edge slats, for much improved maneuverability. It is biased toward the interceptor mission, with provision for a large radar and the big Matra Super 530D missile, being fired here. (Matra)

no doubt that the government will import a weapon or a subsystem if it is too costly to develop in Sweden, and this maintains a competitive element in acquisition. Neither does the Swedish industry try to do everything itself; all Swedish fighters, for example, have had foreign-designed engines and missiles, modified to meet Swedish requirements and produced in Sweden.

The Swedish aerospace industry is dominated by companies that make most of their money building other things. Fighters are built by Saab (the company's full name is Svenska Aeroplan AB; it built aircraft before it built cars) and their engines by Volvo; radars are built by Ericsson, which is a large manufacturer of computers and office equipment. Unlike Northrop, Lockheed or Dassault, these companies do not depend on government contracts in order to survive.

Once plans are made, they are generally adhered to; Sweden is the only nation that has never canceled an aircraft program between first flight and production, and in fact has never had to scrap a project after first cutting metal. Having decided, in

After the French government canceled Dassault's ACF project in 1975, the company built a scaled-up version of the Mirage 2000 with its own money. The Mirage Super 4000, in the background of this photograph, was tested extensively and provided much of the technology for the smaller, more advanced Rafale prototype, in the foreground. Dassault's canards have relatively small foreplanes, set very close to the main wings. (Dassault)

1964, to produce the Saab 37 Viggen first as an attack aircraft, then as a reconnaissance type and finally as a fighter, the Swedes did precisely that, introducing the JA37 interceptor in 1979. The twists and turns in British or US planning over the same period would fill several books.

The question of replacing the Viggen began to require action in the late 1970s; a start had to be made by 1980 if the new aircraft was to enter service in 1992, by which time the older AJ 37 attack aircraft would be needing replacement. After looking very hard at the possibility of developing an improved attack Viggen, the A20, to be combined with a small subsonic strike/reconnaissance aircraft called the Saab 38, the Swedish government decided that the Viggen should be replaced by a supersonic multirole fighter. In mid-1981, an industry working group presented the government with a proposal for a light fighter, only half the Viggen's size, which would supersede all the different Viggen variants. Go-ahead for development and acquisition of 140 aircraft, designated JAS 39 and named Gripen, was given in May 1982. The first Gripen will fly before the end of 1987, long before the Dassault Rafale B or the Eurofighter EFA, and will enter service five years ahead of either.

Almost in parallel with Sweden, an even smaller nation was preparing its entry into the new-fighter business. Israel Aircraft Industries (IAI) had cut its engineering teeth in the 1960s, carrying out make-do conversion jobs to help the then tiny Israel Defense Force-Air Force (IDF-AF) deter a ring of Soviet-equipped adversaries. From fitting weapon pylons to the IDF's little Magister trainers, IAI graduated to re-engining Super Mysteres. When France refused to deliver Mirage 5 fighters which Israel had ordered, after the June 1967 war, IAI—with help from Israeli intelligence—put a copy of the Mirage into production, as the Nesher. The next step was to replace the French Atar engine with the General Electric J79, which was more powerful and was available to Israel; the job was difficult, but a prototype of the re-engined Kfir flew in June 1973. It was followed, just over a year later, by the Kfir-C2, with aerodynamic modifications to improve maneuverability. A more powerful and better-equipped version, the Kfir-C7 entered service in 1983.

Before that time, however, the Israeli government had decided to distill IAI's demonstrated design skill and the IDF-AF's unparalleled combat experience into an all-new aircraft. Designed to replace the Kfir, and later the F-16, it has emerged as the IAI Lavi (Lion). On December 31, 1986, the first Lavi took off from Ben-Gurion airport at Tel-Aviv. This aircraft was not a single prototype, but the first of six full-scale development aircraft built on production tools. The future of the program is not entirely certain but the IDF-AF is expected to take delivery of production aircraft in 1990. (Late in August 1987, as this book closed for press, the Lavi program was canceled for economic reasons.)

Two or possibly three more contenders may yet join the race. Hindustan Aeronautics Limited (HAL) of India is developing a Light Combat Aircraft (LCA) similar in size to the Gripen, also with a single uprated F404. Yugoslavia has a project known as the Novy Avion (New Aircraft), in the same class, which will also move ahead in mid-1987. Both aircraft are likely to fly in the early 1990s. Japan, meanwhile, was considering the launch of a new fighter, called FS-X, but may elect to produce an advanced version of the F-16 or F-18 instead.

These aircraft are not only close in time scale, but they also share many design features, of which the most immediately obvious is their general configuration. Each has a delta wing (albeit modified in different ways) and a pair of all-moving control surfaces ahead of the wing. Tail-first configurations are as old as aviation—the Wright Flyer was designed that way—and the French pioneers who dominated aviation in 1905–10 nicknamed such aircraft "ducks" or *canards*. The name has stuck, both for the general configuration and the forward wing itself.

As Groucho Marx might have said: "Why a canard?"

Experimental tail-first aircraft, such as the elegantly named Curtiss XP-55 Ascender, were tried from time to time in the 1930s and 1940s, but signally failed to unseat the conventional layout. In 1957, the USAF selected the North American XB-70 to replace the B-52; the first canard delta, the massive bomber never went into production, but its configuration was not among its problems. In fact, the existence of the B-70 probably encouraged the resourceful Swedes to adopt a canard delta layout for the Saab 37 Viggen, which became the first canard to enter production after seventy years of experiments.

The basic advantage of the canard is that a foreplane works by lifting the nose of the aircraft, while a conventional stabilizer works by pushing down on the tail. This negative lift is called "trim drag" and can be quite substantial. However, there are problems as well, associated with making the aircraft stable and safe to fly. In the Viggen and the B-70, the aircraft's center of gravity was well forward of the center of lift on the main wing, so that the foreplane carried a great deal of the aircraft's weight in

British Aerospace's Experimental Aircraft Prototype (EAP) is seen just after assembly in October 1985. The black areas of the fuselage, foreplanes and wings are carbon-fiber composite (CFC) material; a production aircraft would use more CFC in the center fuselage and fin.

level flight. If the aircraft was deliberately stalled, or brought up to the point where the wing and foreplane lift began to break down, the foreplane would stall first and the aircraft would pitch down to a stable attitude. Conventional elevons were used to control the aircraft in pitch, to ensure that the foreplane itself could not drive the aircraft into a main-wing-first stall—which would be catastrophic, because the rear of the aircraft would drop and the aircraft would probably not be able to recover.

The common feature of the B-70 and Viggen, which justified their canard layouts, was their requirement for unusual amounts of trim and high lift. The B-70 canard was the only way to get such a heavy delta off the ground at a reasonable speed. The Viggen was required to operate from the 500 meter stretches of hardened roadway that the Swedish Air Force would use instead of runways in wartime. With flaps lowered on the foreplane, and with the foreplane acting rather like a slat on the main wing, the Viggen could approach the runway somewhat slowly and—unlike a conventional delta—in a reasonably flat attitude. However, the Viggen was not particularly agile.

What changed the outlook for the canard was a newer technology, known as "fly-by-wire" or FBW. The controls of high-performance aircraft are driven by small, powerful hydraulic actuators. Until the 1970s, the valves that control the flow of high-pressure fluid to the actuators were opened and closed by steel cables or metal rods, mechanically linked to the pilot's stick and rudder pedals.

Most military aircraft had automatic flight control systems (FCS), incorporating gyroscopes and electronic controls, which were also linked mechanically to the control rods or pulleys and could maintain the aircraft in straight and level flight or steer it according to instructions from the navigation system. Some aircraft had an extra "black box" called a stability augmentation system (SAS), which would sense if the air-

The EAP has a ventral inlet, like the F-16 and Lavi, but the inlet is split because there are two engines. It can be seen that there is plenty of room for internal fuel above the inlet ducts. The large air brakes are positioned to produce a small upward pitching force as they extend, a desirable quality. (BAe)

craft was departing from a preprogrammed envelope of controlled flight and immediately correct it.

The most complex and advanced system of this era was fitted to the Lockheed A-12 reconnaissance aircraft and its descendants, the YF-12 and SR-71 Blackbird. These aircraft were unstable at their Mach 3-plus maximum speeds, and relied completely on the SAS to avoid a departure in pitch and yaw. Individual computers could not be relied on for the job, so the pitch and yaw SAS each had three separate channels; if one computer gave a false reading, a comparator would spot the difference and shut down the channel that disagreed with the other two. If a second failure of this sort occurred, however, the comparator could not tell which of the two remaining channels had failed, so the safety of the system was degraded by a single failure.

In principle, the SAS worked by setting bounds to the flight envelope, and it was of limited use to the fighter designer. As far back as the 1940s, however, some designers had considered a different approach to the entire FCS. Because high-

The EAP is fitted with RB.199 engines, as used on the Tornado. One advantage of a canard is that the afterbody can be structurally and aerodynamically simple, because there is no need to carry horizontal stabilizer loads around the engine bay. (BAe)

performance aircraft were reaching a point where the controls could no longer be moved by manual effort alone, they investigated whether it might make sense to abandon the control rods and cables in favor of electrically operated valves, controlled by electronic signals carried by wires. Early FBW systems were used on the North American A-5 Vigilante and the Concorde supersonic airliner.

With the electronics revolution of the late 1960s, FBW came into its own. Electronic components were now so much smaller, less expensive and more reliable, that the functions of a complex high-authority SAS could be duplicated on a fighter aircraft. For the first time, it was possible to build a fighter that would be unstable under certain circumstances, because the computers would make tiny corrections to the flight path and attitude many times every second. However, a conventional mechanical signaling system could not respond fast enough to match the speed of the computer, so electronic signaling—FBW—was adopted.

The first fighters to combine SAS and FBW were the F-16 and Panavia Tornado, but the F-16 was the first to rely on it totally, by eliminating any mechanical backup from the system. Instead, its FCS had four channels, so that, after one channel had failed and been cut off, the system's "voting logic" would still be able to detect and isolate a second faulty channel; this is called fail-operational-squared design.

The next step in the evolution of FBW was the replacement of analog electronics, as used in the F-16, with digital systems. The difference between the two is fundamental. An analog system deals directly with changing voltages, currents and frequencies; a digital device reduces all inputs to a stream of binary numbers, processes them in that form and reconverts them to a physically measurable output. The rules by which the processing is done are another set of numbers, called software.

By changing the software in the FBW system, it can be made to respond in different ways; for example, it can react automatically to the way the aircraft is loaded, so

The EAP on its first flight, carrying Sky Flash and AIM-132 ASRAAM missile mockups. The complex twist of the wing, maintained at high flight loads by aeroelastic tailoring, is apparent here, as are the large two-section leading-edge flaps. (BAe)

the pilot barely notices if the aircraft is carrying a heavy payload. A digital system can also communicate more easily with the other systems aboard the aircraft. In fact, the advances in electronic design over the past twenty years have mostly concerned digital systems. In 1958, for instance, the Convair F-106 was famous as the first fighter to have a real, gee-whiz digital computer on board; a modern fighter has dozens. Cost, maintainability and reliability all favor the digital FBW system.

What happens frequently in technological development is that the first use of a new device, such as FBW, proves that the system works. The next generation of applications can be designed with full knowledge of how the system works, and can be designed from the ground up to take maximum advantage of it. This is what has happened with the new canard fighters.

With FBW to take care of stability, the new fighters have been designed so that most of the lift is carried on the main wing—the larger and more efficient lifting surface—in level, subsonic flight. At supersonic speed, the center of lift on the main wing moves aft, and the canard is used to provide an upward trimming force. (Trim drag becomes very significant on a tail-aft aircraft at such speeds, and even more so in supersonic maneuvering flight.) At low speeds, the canard balances out the strong

The unusual location of the EAP foreplane was selected to cause the least possible interference with the pilot's view while maintaining the correct aerodynamic relationship between the foreplane and the wing. The fighter's compact profile is typical of canard configurations with a high usable volume in a small airframe. (BAe)

nose-down pitch caused by the trailing-edge flaps, enabling the new canard fighters to land slowly and in a flat attitude.

Another feature of the new canard fighter is that the foreplane is very close in plan-view to the main wing. The aerodynamic effects are favorable—the foreplane tends to act as a slat for the mainplane, as on the Viggen—but a most important advantage is that it becomes possible to have a long-chord delta-type wing without the long and heavy fuselage previously needed to carry the stabilizing surface.

The new aircraft have delta, or modified delta wings. Deltas have their advantages, as the Mirage series and the Kfir have shown, but these have previously been offset by drawbacks. Characteristically, classic deltas have been known for being able to pull hard turns for a few seconds, before the high drag caused by their short span, and the high trim drag caused by the short lever arm of their elevons slow them down. (The elevons of a conventional delta are close to the fulcrum of the aircraft, and have to push down hard to trim it.) The modern deltas, however, have leading-edge flaps for high lift at moderate angles of attack, compound sweep (in some cases) and longer span for reduced drag, and canards to handle trim and control. They also take full advantage of recent advances in aerodynamic design, using powerful computers to optimize both the planform and section of the wing for low drag over a wide flight envelope.

The main point in favor of the delta is its long chord. Because the ratio of thickness to chord is an important factor in drag at high speed, a conventional high-speed wing is very shallow; the much longer delta can be much thicker. Its spars are deeper and hence stronger in relation to their weight, and it has a great deal of fuel volume. The delta also provides much more undersurface area for mounting weapons; while a conventional fighter such as the F-18 carries two Sparrow or AMRAAMs (advanced medium-range air-to-air missiles) on its fuselage, the canard-delta EAP can carry four, efficiently sunken into its long wing root. Larger weapons, such as bombs, can be carried in tandem rows on short pylons, instead of being mounted in draggy clusters on heavy multiple racks.

The canard delta seems to be a very attractive configuration for a fighter. Area Ruling demands that a supersonic fighter have a long nose, wherever the horizontal stabilizer is located. The canard delta is little longer ahead of the wing than conventional fighters, and has nothing but the jetpipes behind it, giving it a stubby, pugnacious look and saving a considerable amount of weight. The afterbody design is also cleaner, with the horizontal stabilizer out of the way.

The advantages of the canard delta are most obvious in the Lavi and Gripen. Lower drag, higher lift and more efficient weapons carriage have been translated, in both cases, into smaller size and lower cost. The Lavi's modified-delta wing spans only 28 ft. 7 in., less than the span of Cessna 150, and its empty weight is 15,305 pounds, but it can take off for a long-range attack mission at a weight of 42,000 pounds—that is, with a load of fuel and weapons equal to 175 percent of its empty weight.

The Gripen is even smaller. Its single Volvo/General Electric RM12 engine is a derivative of the F404, two of which power the F-18, but it is still designed to carry a pair of heavy antishipping missiles or up to six air-to-air missiles, four of them being

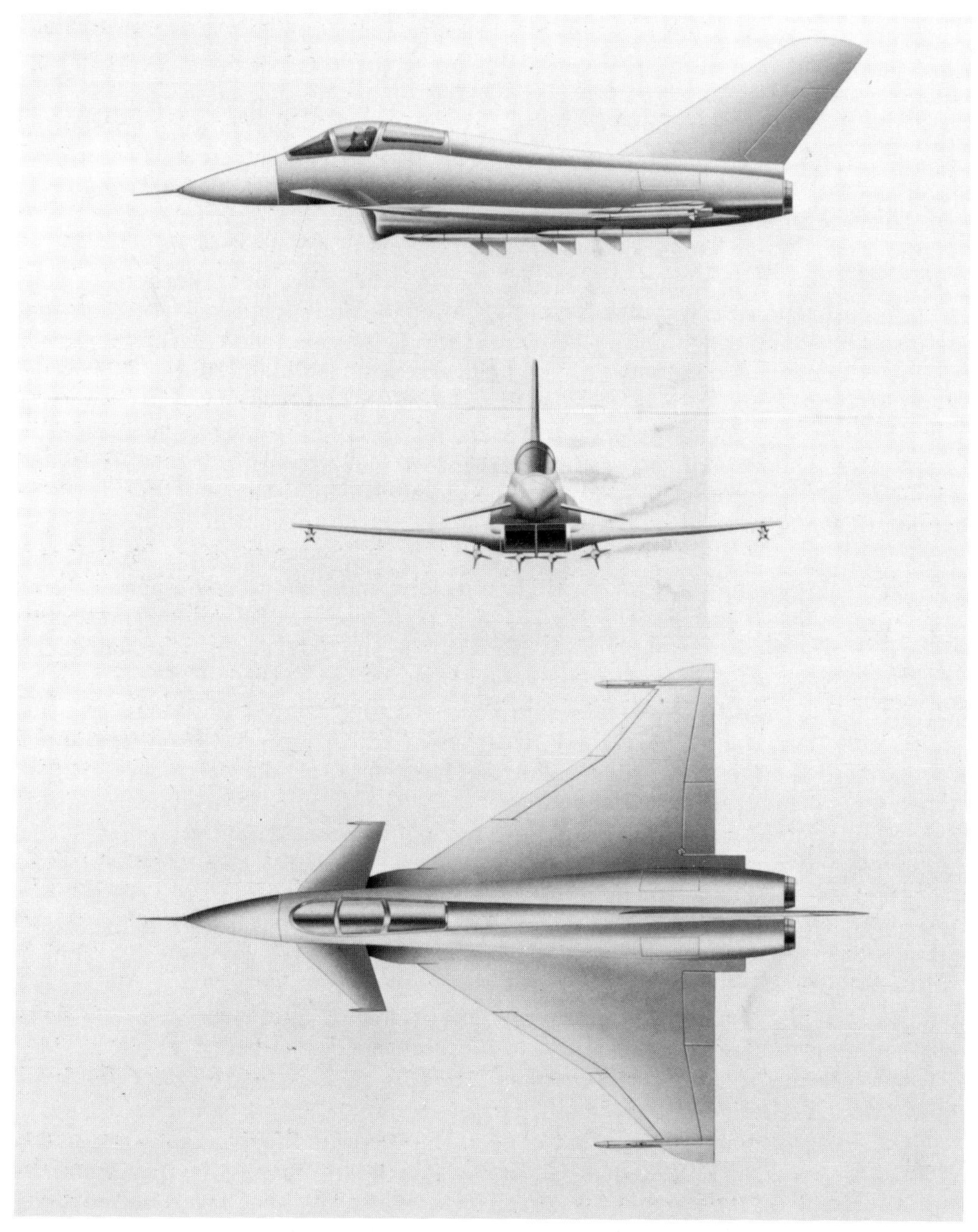

Three-view drawing of the EAP shows that the wing planform recalls that of the fighter's distant relative, the Concorde supersonic transport. Both use vortex-flow aerodynamics to alleviate some disadvantages of the classic delta wing. (BAe)

500 pound Rb71 Sky Flash medium-range weapons. Among current service fighters, only the big and expensive F-14 and F-15 can carry more than two medium-range AAMs.

The four new canard deltas are also similar in the materials used in their construction. Again, a technology embodied in earlier designs—in this case, composite material—is now being fully exploited in the latest generation of aircraft.

Composite material gets its name from the fact that it comprises two distinct elements: fibers, with high tensile strength, and a matrix, or a glue which bonds the fibers together into a structure that resists compression. The most familiar composite material, because it occurs in nature, is wood, and the earliest example of an all-composite military aircraft was the de Havilland Mosquito of World War II.

Around that same time, the first artificial composite material was developed, using glass fibers in a matrix made of epoxy resin—an artificial glue first used on the Mosquito. Fiberglass proved versatile and strong, and has been widely used for light aircraft, small boats and cars such as the Corvette, but it cannot be used for highly loaded structures such as fighter airframes because it is too elastic; under flight loads, it would bend and flutter.

In the 1960s, British researchers found how to make fibers out of almost pure carbon, essentially by "cooking" filaments of artificial fiber. Carbon fibers were stronger than glass, and much less elastic, and, with an epoxy-resin matrix, could be made into a material substantially stronger in relation to its weight than aluminum.

Known as graphite-epoxy or simply graphite in the United States, carbon-fiber composite (CFC) materials are now widely used throughout the aircraft industry. The first military aircraft to use CFC on a large scale were the F-18, which had CFC wing skins and access panels, and the AV-8B, which had an all-CFC wing. The British Aerospace EAP prototype, however, shows once again how a technology can be used more boldly when its basic characteristics have been proven.

CFC is delivered to the aircraft manufacturer in the form of sheets or rolls of fabric, preimpregnated with resin and known as "pre-preg." Most of the fibers run in one direction (warp) with just enough cross fibers *(weft)* to hold the material together. The cloth is cut to the shape of the component, usually with a high-pressure (several thousand pounds per square inch) jet of water, mixed with a hard abrasive powder. Composite material would dull any blade as quickly as paper dulls scissors. It is then stacked in many layers to form the three-dimensional shape of the component and "cured" under heat and pressure in an autoclave. The resin in the different layers fuses together, and they become, for practical purposes, one piece.

This process gives the manufacturer some options that do not exist with conventional materials. For example, the designer specifies, in the laying-up process, in which direction the warp of the individual layers will run. In the case of a component such as a wing skin, most of the fibers would usually run parallel to the long axis of the wing, because that is where the greatest loads occur. If the warp is at an angle to the structural axis, however, a phenomenon occurs that is familiar to fashion designers and tailors; the material tends to shear, so that a bending load is translated into a twisting movement. It follows then, that if the aircraft designer can orient the right number of the long fibers in the right direction, the way the wing twists under load can be controlled.

Appropriately, this process is called "aeroelastic tailoring." On a swept wing, for example, the wing twists upward under load, reducing the incidence of the outer wing, and reducing the amount of lift it can generate. To produce more lift, the whole wing has to operate at a sharper angle to the air, increasing its drag. But if the structure can be made *not* to twist, the wing continues to develop lift along its entire span, as it should do for maximum efficiency. The EAP's highly twisted wing not only embodies new aerodynamic technology, but it also uses aeroelastic tailoring to maintain those qualities over the entire flight envelope.

This combination of the canard configuration with aeroelastic tailoring and digital flight control should produce fighters that are not only fast and agile, but that are as well mannered as the classic thoroughbred fighters of the past. As the service-entry date of the EFA and Rafale B has moved toward 1995, however, European designers must be watching, with some nervousness, the progress of a highly ambitious project on the other side of the Atlantic: the US Air Force's Advanced Tactical Fighter.

Chapter 3

Advanced tactical fighter

No air force in the world is organized quite like the US Air Force. Almost all the way up the organizational chart, the service is divided into influential and, in many respects, autonomous commands. And while officers may transfer from one command to another for a short time, the path to promotion is primarily straight and vertical. The system concentrates experience and talent, generates intense loyalty to the command and its mission, and fosters an internal culture within each command that transcends any year-by-year shifts of policy and changes of emphasis.

Tactical Air Command (TAC) is the operator of all the USAF's fighter, attack and tactical reconnaissance aircraft based in the continental United States, and is responsible for supplying combat-ready fighting units to the US Air Forces in Europe and the Pacific. TAC is, therefore, a fighter pilot's service, and virtually all its senior officers, in any function, are current or former fighter pilots.

The result is that TAC's internal culture favors the mission that fighter pilots themselves favor: aggressive air-to-air combat, intended to destroy large numbers of enemy aircraft and to prevent the enemy from carrying out air attacks on ground forces. This mission is identified in TAC jargon as "air superiority" or "counter-air."

Soldiers and military reformers may argue that TAC should spend more time and effort on air-to-ground missions, but it is hard to convince a fighter commander that the destruction of a $100,000 tank warrants exposing a $25 million fighter to the risk of being shot down by a $5,000 missile. Politicians, the Pentagon and the senior USAF command did manage to put the A-10 Warthog tankbuster into TAC in the 1970s, but the fighter pilot culture has proved more enduring than the tenure of senior commanders, and the slow, hit-susceptible "Hog" is on its way to premature retirement. Once again, TAC's philosophy of warfare rests heavily on causing massive attrition of enemy air forces in air-to-air combat before assigning the bulk of the force to air-to-ground missions.

In 1944–45 over Europe, and 1950–53 over Korea, US fighter pilots enjoyed a degree of superiority in equipment and training, which made an excellent match with this philosophy. The North American P-51D Mustang had a heavy armament, protective features such as pilot armor and self-sealing tanks, and speed and maneuverability that compared well with any of its adversaries. It also had a greater range than almost any contemporary fighter, so the US fighter pilots could roam at will over Western Europe. Their German opponents, flying shorter-legged Fw190s and Bf109s, were confined to the defense of specific targets, and could seldom concentrate enough aircraft in one area to effectively oppose a P-51 incursion.

In 1945, North American designers naturally proposed a jet-powered fighter loosely based on the P-51 design. Before work started on the prototype, the ransacking of German research centers yielded a wealth of data on swept-back wings, and such a wing was incorporated into the new fighter, the XP-86. As the F-86A Sabre, the new fighter achieved at least a 4:1 kill ratio against MiG-15s over North Korea, partly because of superior range and speed (which, once again, gave the US pilots the initiative and opportunity to engage when conditions were in their favor), and partly because of refinements such as powdered ailerons and a radar gunsight. The latter, like

This group of Lockheed studies, from the late 1970s and early 1980s, show some of the many and varied concepts that may be examined before a new fighter requirement takes shape. This remarkable fighter seaplane recalls the Convair Sea Dart of the 1950s; one advantage of such an aircraft would be that its "runway" would be hard for an enemy to damage. (Lockheed)

the gyroscopic predictor gunsight before it, was initially scorned as a gimmick, but the USAF had learned early on that very few good pilots were also outstanding marksmen and that any aid to gunnery was valuable.

Planners and designers lost sight of the classic fighter virtues among the wonders of missiles and electronics in the 1950s, but the fighter-pilot culture endured. The young pilots of Korea became the front-line commanders of Vietnam, and, as the generals of the 1970s, they put the F-15 and F-16 into service. The F-15, in particular, takes on the mission of the P-51 and F-86. With a 700 mile combat radius, eight-missile armament and a lavish equipment list including a powerful radar and internal electronic warfare system, the F-15 is a formidable opponent which, in Israeli hands, has destroyed almost sixty MiG-21s and MiG-23s, together with a brace of Mach 3

A highly maneuverable short-takeoff-and-landing (STOL) fighter, also studied by Lockheed. The configuration allows the vectoring engine nozzles to be placed close to the center of gravity, so that they can make the largest possible contribution to lift without unbalancing the aircraft. (Lockheed)

With a strong background in supersonic cruise technology, Lockheed tended to favor such an approach to fighter requirements in the 1980s. This impression was produced to illustrate Lockheed's response in 1982 to US Navy plans for a multirole fighter, known as VFMX. The program did not go ahead, however. (Lockheed)

This very exotic Lockheed study reflected some work on "compression lift" in which supersonic shock waves are exploited to provide lift without a commensurate increase in drag. In this case, the shock waves shed by the fuselage are trapped under the high-mounted, drooped wing, in the same way that the spike or splitter of a supersonic air inlet interacts with the inlet wall. (Lockheed)

MiG-25s, without a single loss in air-to-air combat. That is the kind of exchange ratio a fighter pilot can live with.

Fighter development in the United States is a continuous process. As one new aircraft completes its development and goes into service with TAC, the end of another's service life, or the end of its dominance over its potential adversaries, may be in sight or another gap may have opened up in the fleet. This was the situation in the late 1970s, as the F-16 followed the F-15 into service.

TAC is an aircraft operator, however, and does not develop aircraft. That is the responsibility of the Aeronautical Systems Division (ASD) of the Air Force's Systems Command. In its many incarnations since the 1920s, ASD has been based at Wright-Patterson AFB, a few minutes out of Dayton, Ohio, the home of Orville and Wilbur Wright. The user commands such as TAC often refer to ASD as "The Bicycle Shop," referring to the Wrights' trade, and communicating the front-line pilots' sometimes skeptical view of those who live in a world of technical tinkering.

ASD is not only responsible for managing current aircraft and engine programs, but also for ensuring that both it and the industry are ready with technology to meet future requirements as they arise. It is impossible to predict exactly what these requirements will be, let alone how they will be met. So ASD works to identify the most likely requirements, distill them to a range of options, and develop technology that is

Lockheed's response to the first USAF "request for information" on the Advanced Tactical Fighter was this Mach 3, 120,000-pound aircraft capable of interception or strike missions. Vectoring engine nozzles would be used to improve its maneuver performance and, in conjunction with retractable foreplanes, to give the aircraft STOL characteristics. (Lockheed)

generally applicable to all or most of them. As the need for a new system approaches, ASD and the user command gradually eliminate and narrow the options, long before the USAF commits itself to full-scale development. In the case of something as important and as staggeringly expensive as a new fighter, that process takes many years.

The USAF's first thoughts about the next new fighter, in 1978 and 1979, were not centered on an F-15 replacement. The service had a more pressing requirement: it was short of long-range strike aircraft, which it needed to attack enemy airfields, roads, bridges and railway junctions and thereby impede the land battle. Because of cost overruns and technical problems with the F-111, which had been designed specifically to do this, the USAF had been left with less than 500 of the 1,000-plus F-111s it had originally wanted, but there were as many targets as ever.

The late 1970s were also a time of great concern about events in the Middle East. Upon the collapse of the "made-in-America" imperial regime in Iran, in 1979, the Pentagon in general and the USAF in particular realized that US air coverage of any conflict in that area would be marginal, simply because of range. Designed with the much smaller European central area in mind, the F-16 and F-15 would be much more limited at longer ranges. On combat air patrol missions, they would be able to stay on station for less time during each sortie, and they would carry fewer weapons on strike missions. Each sortie would accordingly be less productive, and it would take more aircraft to accomplish the same task.

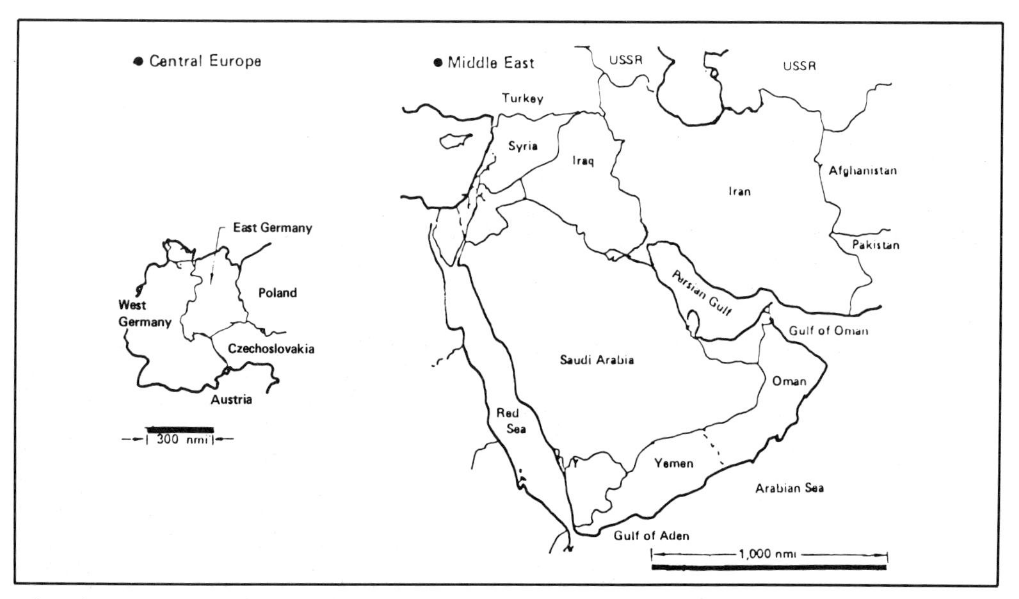

After the Iranian revolution of 1979 and the Soviet invasion of Afghanistan, the USAF began to look very seriously at the problems of operations in the Southwest Asian theater. The main challenge is range, as these maps show. (Boeing)

Early in the ATF design process, the balance between air-to-air and air-to-surface missions was not fixed. This study, from Boeing, strongly emphasizes ground attack; with its dorsal inlets and variable-sweep wings, it bears some resemblance to the aircraft that Boeing designed for the TFX competition in the early 1960s, and was the runner-up to the F-111. (Boeing)

Later, Boeing's attention turned to a single-seat canard-delta configuration with advanced multisegment wing flaps. Large air-to-surface weapons are carried in ventral troughs, to reduce their contribution to the aircraft's drag and radar image. (Boeing)

In 1983, the USAF decided to bias the ATF requirement toward air-to-air combat while using a developed version of an existing fighter to attack ground targets. One reason for this was that systems mounted in external pods could be used to turn an air-to-air fighter into a bomber. The LANTIRN (low altitude navigation and targeting by infrared at night) pods attached to this F-16 incorporate infrared sensors, a laser designator and a terrain-following radar. (USAF)

General Dynamics' F-16XL prototypes were produced by modifying standard F-16s with new "arrow" wings. Compared with a conventional delta, the arrow wing has greater span and is more efficient at low speeds; it can hold a tremendous amount of internal fuel, and provides space for external stores. (General Dynamics)

But moving more aircraft was also difficult, simply because of the number of people and the tonnage of equipment needed to support them. The F-15 was a particular problem in this respect. Its complex electronics were designed so that problems could be quickly fixed on the flight line by removing a defective box or module and substituting a new one. But the modules themselves were too large and costly to be discarded or returned to a major depot every time they malfunctioned, so the USAF provided each F-15 unit with an Avionics Intermediate Shop (AIS) where faults could be traced to a specific component within the module. But the AIS, which was essential if the unit was to sustain operations, took four C-141 freighters to carry it, a quarter of the total support requirement for each unit.

The first substantial step toward developing a new fighter was taken in June 1981, when ASD issued a "request for information" (RFI). An RFI has unofficially been described by an ASD officer as "a way of getting industry to pay for our studies." It does not call for any detailed design work, but usually seeks opinions on what features are feasible, desirable or cost-effective for a new system, given its mission, the threat and a desired service-entry date. The June 1981 RFI asked for views on a new aircraft, called the Advanced Tactical Fighter (ATF), with a deadline of August 1982 for replies.

Instead of using heavy, inefficient multiple bomb racks, the F-16XL was designed to carry bombs in tandem rows on short single pylons. The nose of a dummy AIM-120 missile can be seen under the wing root; the F-16XL could carry four AIM-120s and two wingtip-mounted AIM-9s as well as a full load of bombs. (General Dynamics)

The USAF made the fewest possible specific requirements in the RFI, to encourage the manufacturers to think of ideas on their own. However, ASD told the industry to consider costs, logistics and the threat—both in terms of SAMs and fighters, and in terms of antiairfield weapons. However, even ASD was quite surprised by the diversity of responses. Lockheed-California proposed what one USAF officer called a "battle cruiser," weighing 120,000 pounds and cruising at more than Mach 3; Northrop's design weighed less than a quarter as much. While some of the designs were deltas, McDonnell Douglas' design had an ultra-thin-section straight wing, and Grumman proposed a swing-wing type.

However, there was some general agreement, summed up by a McDonnell Douglas paper that emphasized "STOL, Stealth and supercruise" as the most important attributes for a new fighter. All of them represented major advances over the F-15 or any other contemporary fighter.

STOL stands for short-takeoff and landing. Modern fighters such as the F-16 and F-15 have lots of power and big wings in proportion to their weight, and can take off in a reasonably short distance. On landing, these assets turn into liabilities. The big engine is unresponsive at low thrust, and the big wing makes the aircraft very susceptible to pitch changes, so the modern fighter is tricky to fly at low speeds. This makes it difficult for pilots to land at a precise point on the runway, particularly if exhausted from combat. Once on the ground, the aircraft takes a long time to slow down. Brakes can accomplish only so much, particularly on a wet runway, and while braking parachutes are sometimes effective, they are tricky in crosswinds. The net result is that contemporary fighters still need more than 8,000 feet of concrete for unrestricted safe operations.

STOL, however, is one of the few effective counters to the danger from antirunway weapons. STOL gives the commander the ability to disperse his aircraft away

McDonnell Douglas fitted the F-15 with conformal fuel tanks (visible here as bulges beside the engine nacelles) to improve its range at low level for the strike mission. Weapon pylons attached to the tanks carry bombs more efficiently than multiple underwing racks. (McDonnell Douglas)

from the main base, but, more importantly, it allows the fighters to operate from taxiways and perimeter tracks, and means that repair crews need only fix a short stretch of concrete before aircraft can resume landings.

One bomb crater can disable a 10,000 foot runway if the fighters need 8,000 feet to land in, as long as it hits somewhere within 3,000 feet of the mid-point on the runway. If the fighters need only 2,000 feet, however, the attacker has a much more difficult task; half-a-dozen craters are needed, with near-equal spacing between them. USAF specialists looked at their data, and decided that as long as the ATF could land in less than 2,000 feet, and as long as repair crews could fix two to three craters an hour, an all-out attack on airfields would reduce sortie rates by only twenty percent.

Stealth, or the use of measures that make an aircraft less susceptible to detection and tracking, has been widely discussed and reported since the early 1980s, but its tactical implications were only beginning to dawn on many people at the time. When the RFI was issued, only a few small prototype Stealth aircraft, mostly built by Lockheed, had flown. Development of Lockheed's operational Stealth fighter had barely begun, and ASD was preparing to choose between Northrop/Boeing and Lockheed/Rockwell teams as prime contractors on the Stealth bomber. What hard data had been obtained was so highly classified that many of the people involved in ATF studies were not cleared to know about it. While most people felt that Stealth would be valuable, there was definitely some doubt in 1982 as to whether it could be achieved on a high-performance aircraft.

The first McDonnell Douglas F-15E flew in December 1986. With two seats, LANTIRN pods and a very powerful radar, it is an extremely effective multirole fighter. Its maximum takeoff weight is no less than twice the F-15's original design TOW of 40,000 pounds. (McDonnell Douglas)

The AFTI/F-16, distinguished from the standard aircraft by its dorsal spine and downward-angled foreplanes under the inlet duct, was the first of a series of prototypes which demonstrated key ATF technologies. The AFTI/F-16 was used to evaluate unconventional flight control techniques, new weapon-aiming concepts and cockpit voice recognition. (USAF)

In another AFTI program, this F-111 has been fitted with a "mission-adaptive" wing. Instead of conventional flaps, the AFTI/F-111 has flexible leading and trailing edges, with complex actuators that deflect them along a smooth curve. An automatic control system operates the flaps to reduce drag, increase performance and reduce structural loads. (Boeing)

Supercruise, also known as supersonic persistence, means the ability to sustain supersonic speed without using afterburning, which no current fighter can do in normal service. As a result, supersonic speed is available for no more than a few minutes in any sortie. It was more firmly established on the requirements list than Stealth, because it was considered essential if TAC was to maintain its ability to conduct aggressive fighter operations over hostile territory. Surface-to-air missiles (SAMs) are probably the most important threat in this regime. Even if the intruding fighters can escape destruction or damage by SAMs, they are unlikely to accomplish their mission if they must constantly change course to avoid the lethal envelopes of SAM systems, maintain electronic silence to avoid detection and periodically use afterburner to avoid missile attacks.

The USAF decided ATF should fly at about Mach 1.4–1.5 (930–1,000 mph) on dry thrust with full armament, and cruise at a greater altitude than current fighters: 70,000 feet as opposed to 50,000 feet. This would eliminate smaller SAMs from the picture, and shrink the lethal envelopes of larger SAM systems, because they can cover much less area at higher altitudes. At supersonic speed, covering the ground some seventy-five percent faster than a subsonic-cruise type, the advanced fighter would cross the shrunken danger zone more quickly. The combination of higher cruise altitude and speed could reduce the fighter's exposure time by a factor of three. The reduction in the SAM system's kill probability (P_k) might be even greater, because the SAM is least maneuverable and most likely to fail to follow its target at the extreme upper edge of its envelope. This "high-fast sanctuary," as tactical analysts call it, has been successfully exploited for years by the A-12 and SR-71. By 1981, advances in aerodynamics and propulsion were making it possible for this performance to be combined with conventional fighter virtues.

The AFTI/F-111 in cruising flight, with the wings at an intermediate camber setting. At supersonic speeds, the camber would be further reduced to minimize drag. Work on technology programs such as this put Boeing, which had never built a supersonic aircraft or a jet fighter, in an unexpectedly strong position in the contest to develop ATF. (Boeing)

The Bicycle Shop experts evaluated the first responses to the RFI and presented their conclusions at a meeting in Anaheim, California, in October 1982. The outlines of today's ATF emerged quite clearly: a supersonic-cruise aircraft, with a combat radius of 700–920 miles (a significant increase over the F-15), and with reduced observables if possible. It would be able to take off from a 2,000 foot runway and have the ability to taxi over roughly repaired surfaces, and it would be easier to support than the F-15.

The USAF's conclusions on weight, given the wide diversity among the RFI responses, were very significant. At the upper end of the size scale, the ATF became too expensive, and the service could not buy enough aircraft to cover all the targets. At the lower end, the more demanding missions could only be carried out with the use of external fuel tanks, which made supersonic persistence questionable and made Stealth unattainable. The requirements balanced, the USAF felt, at about 60,000 pounds for an aircraft optimized for air-to-air missions, and about 80,000 pounds if the ATF was designed for the strike role.

It was also clear that the ATF would push the state of the art very hard in several different areas, and that the USAF and industry were far from ready to start a full-scale

The most radical prototype to foreshadow ATF is the Grumman X-29 forward-swept-wing (FSW) aircraft. FSW technology promises improvements in maneuverability and efficiency for future fighters, according to its advocates. Also visible here are the X-29's all-moving foreplanes, its variable-camber trailing-edge flaps and the "strake flaps" on the extreme tail. (Grumman)

The black CFC skins of the X-29's wings are visible in this view of the first aircraft under construction in 1983. The structure is extremely dense, even with the use of aeroelastic tailoring. The forward fuselage is that of the fifteenth Northrop F-5A fighter, originally built in the mid-1960s. (Grumman)

development program; the uncertainties and risks were too great. However, the USAF had anticipated this problem, and its approach to the ATF program represented a break with previous practice.

In the early days of military aircraft, there was no such thing as a "weapon system" or a "program." The P-51 and F-86, for example, were designed as complete aircraft, using the best engines and other equipment available. With the exception of the engine, all the vital parts were designed by the manufacturer or bought off the shelf, and if one part was not ready on time, another could be substituted.

In December 1949, North American flew a new version of the Sabre, the F-86D, which was to help change the way military aircraft were produced. The F-86D had a radar and fire control computer, without which the pilot could not aim its rocket armament. But the radar was not ready as the fighters started to roll off the produc-

Due to fly early in 1988, the F-15 STOL Maneuver Technology Demonstrator (SMTD) should help designers build an ATF which can land in 1,500 feet or less under any weather conditions, without detriment to its performance or maneuverability. This impression shows the F-15 SMTD on approach; its engine nozzles are almost completely closed, and all thrust is being delivered through movable cascade vanes above and below the fuselage. (McDonnell Douglas)

tion line, and for a while there were more than 100 brand-new F-86Ds parked at the factory, useless because they had no radars. Experience on the Northrop F-89 Scorpion heavy all-weather fighter was even worse; by the time the last aircraft completed their last modification program to make them service-ready, the type was obsolete, and a few F-89s were delivered directly from the modification line to the USAF's storage facility at Davis-Monthan AFB, in Arizona.

As a result of these and other embarrassing problems, the Pentagon decided that future aircraft would be developed as weapon systems. For each aircraft, the USAF would form a program management office, an organization that would be responsible for every part of the aircraft, its weapons, all the equipment and facilities on the ground that the aircraft would need, and all the documentation and training manuals associated with the hardware. To keep the development period for such a large task down to a reasonable level, preparations for production were to be made concurrently with the detail design of the system.

This system worked much better than no system at all, but was not perfect. New weapons continued to have problems, and would often reach the Air Force late, overpriced, overweight or underdeveloped, with shortfalls in reliability and performance. Part of the trouble was momentum; once the program was moving, it was very expensive to hold up production, and managers were usually tempted to plow on, hoping that the technical snags would be cleared up in time. This was very apparent on the F-111, where only the last 100 or so aircraft, the F-111Fs, really met the USAF specification, and the service ended up with five distinctly different versions, a logistical nightmare.

In the long run-up to the ATF program, the USAF recognized two problems with the 1950s management system. First, it did not allow much time for unexpected problems, and it rarely provided for alternative solutions if these problems proved serious. Second, the ideal of concurrency, in which everything was supposed to be taken from the drawing board to production in the same forty-eight or sixty months, did not reflect reality. Some subsystems and technologies simply took longer to mature than others.

The first fruits of this new wisdom were a series of experimental programs that started in the late 1970s, some of them grouped under the heading AFTI (Advanced Fighter Technology Integration). Using modified versions of existing aircraft, or new aircraft with off-the-shelf parts, none of these programs was so expensive as to attract Congressional budget-trimmers. In some cases, too, costs were shared with the National Aeronautics and Space Administration (NASA) or the Defense Advanced Research Projects Agency (DARPA). The overall strategy was to start work first on generic technologies that were widely applicable and likely to be used on almost any new fighter, regardless of its specific performance numbers.

One of the first was the AFTI/F-16, in which a programmable, digital FBW system was installed on a prototype F-16, together with two large fins projecting downward and outward from the forward fuselage. There were several objectives, but the most important was to demonstrate new ways of flying an aircraft in combat. In a conventional aircraft, the responses to the pilot's inputs are "coupled": if the pilot raises the nose, the aircraft will fly up; if he wants to change the aircraft's heading, he must bank. In the AFTI/F-16, though, the forward fins and other surfaces could be used so that part of the maneuver was canceled, and therefore the aircraft could make flat turns, or climb or lose height with the fuselage level. The program started at the end of 1978, and the aircraft flew in July 1982.

While the AFTI/F-16 went on to demonstrate some new and useful technology, one of its main contributions was negative. Although all the systems analyses and computer simulations had shown that decoupled flight modes would be a boon in air combat, the pilots who flew the aircraft found that its strange behavior reminded them of an aircraft on the point of "departing," the pilot's abbreviation for "departing from controlled flight," or, in lay terms, swapping ends.

Another early starter among the technology programs was the AFTI/F-111. This had its distant roots in the Boeing 747 airliner, and its unique flexible leading-edge flap; the flap drops down from the front of the wing, and its actuators curl its front edge into a smooth, aerodynamic shape, fooling the air into thinking that the 747 has a blunt, thick wing.

One of the objectives of the SMTD program is to show that the Pratt & Whitney vectoring/reversing nozzles have advantages in all flight regimes that offset their weight and complexity. As well as increasing maneuverability, reversing nozzles could permit the elimination of large airbrakes from ATF. (McDonnell Douglas)

Some Boeing engineers extrapolated this into a design for a wing with flexible-skinned flaps over its entire leading and trailing edges. Unlike conventional flaps, these could be moved throughout the flight to adapt the wing to whatever speed, altitude and loading conditions were required: hence its name, the Mission Adaptive Wing (MAW). An F-111, previously modified with advanced supercritical wings, was chosen for the program, because its removable wings facilitated modification and it could evaluate the MAW over a very wide flight envelope. Somewhat behind schedule, partly due to the problems of packing a very complex actuation system into a very thin wing, the AFTI/F-111 made its first flight in October 1985.

The benefits of the MAW or a similar "smart-wing" system are considerable. By deflecting the flaps upward or downward, the system can determine what setting gives the lowest drag and the greatest speed for a given power setting. In a hard maneuver, the inboard flaps go down and the outboard flaps remain up, so that the lift is concentrated near the center of the wing, and less brute structural strength is needed to

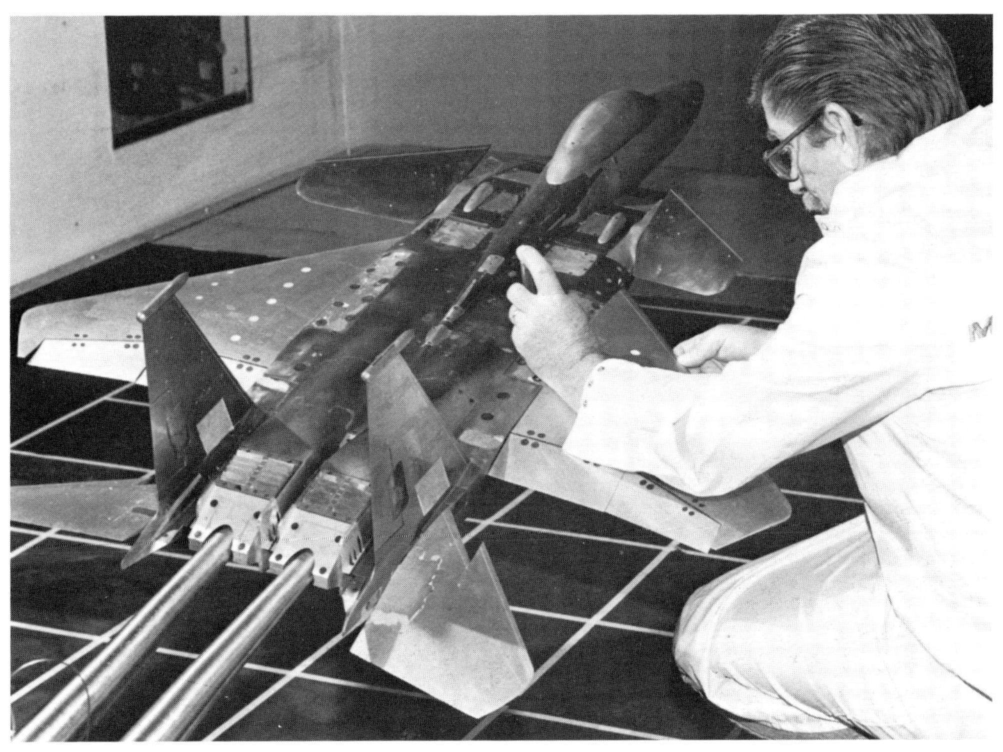

Complex, ultra-accurate wind-tunnel models, such as this F-15 SMTD, are still necessary despite the use of computers for aerodynamic simulation. This model is used for low-speed tests, including investigations of the interaction between the exhaust from the thrust reversers and the airframe. (McDonnell Douglas)

cope with maneuver loads. Therefore, an MAW can be longer and more efficient, lighter or thinner than a conventional "dumb" wing. The smart wing can make the aircraft more responsive to control commands, deflecting quickly downward to start the maneuver before the tail can rotate the aircraft. The MAW was still only halfway through its test program in early 1987, but the technology is a very strong candidate for ATF.

The most visually striking of the aircraft that paved the way to ATF, however, was the radical Grumman X-29, the USAF's forward-swept wing (FSW) demonstrator. The program went back to the mid-1970s, when sustained maneuverability was the most desired quality in a fighter aircraft, and a number of engineers saw that the FSW might be the way to improve it.

The secret lay in the fact that the shock wave on any swept wing, at transonic or supersonic speed, lies on a line roughly seventy percent of the way from the leading edge to the trailing edge; the line is called the "shock sweep." On a swept-back wing with normal taper, most of the wing is swept more sharply than the shock sweep and lies ahead of the shock line, generating suction and drag. With a swept-forward wing,

The F-15 SMTD is intended to fly at speeds where the controls of a conventional F-15 would become ineffective. A pair of F-18 stabilizers, attached to the engine inlet ducts, act as canard foreplanes. They operate together to control the aircraft in pitch. When they move differentially, they create a strong rolling moment and, because they are angled sharply upward, yaw the aircraft as well. (McDonnell Douglas)

the critical zone between the leading edge and the shock line is smaller and more highly loaded, and there is less suction and less drag. Because of the same basic geometrical reasons, the structural box of a swept-forward wing is shorter in relation to the span than that of a conventional wing of similar performance.

The problem, though, is that the aeroelastic characteristics of the FSW—that is, the way it bends under air loads—are unpleasant. If a swept-back wing bends upward at the tips, as any wing will do under load, it twists so that the angle at which the tip strikes the air is reduced. The tip makes less lift, and the bending reaches a stable point and stops.

The FSW is different, however. As the tip bends upward, it twists upward as well, and the only way to stop it from twisting clean off the airplane is to hold it in place by structural force. This would occasion an unacceptable weight penalty for a metal-winged tactical aircraft, but composites, and the new art of aeroelastic tailoring, provided a more elegant solution. If the skins were laid up with some seventy percent of the carbon fibers aligned nine degrees forward of the leading-edge sweep, they would have asymmetrical shearing characteristics. As the wing bent upward, the upper skin, in compression, would shear forward and the lower skin, in tension, would shear aft. But if both skins were clamped to the wing's substructure, the shear resis-

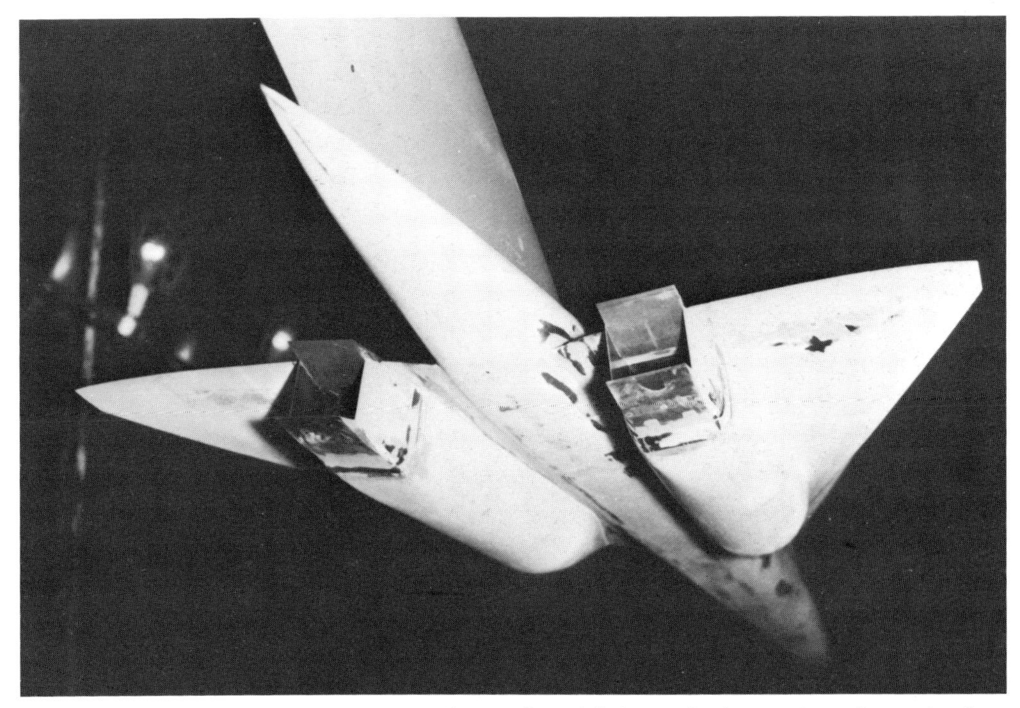

A Boeing wind-tunnel model shows the integration of reversing/vectoring nozzles into a supersonic fighter. (Boeing)

tance of the skins would create a twisting force strong enough to counter the aeroelastic effects.

In the late 1970s, several manufacturers believed that FSW was the wave of the future, and the competition to produce an FSW demonstrator was intense. Grumman was awarded the contract in January 1981, partly because its proposal saved money by using existing hardware, and applied it to demonstrating other new technologies along with the FSW. The two Grumman X-29 prototypes used the fuselages of early-production Northrop F-5A fighters, Honeywell flight control system hardware similar to that developed for the SR-71 (when the Blackbirds were converted to digital FCS in the early 1980s), off-the-shelf F404 engines and a host of minor components from the F-16.

As was the FSW, the X-29 was designed with a thin, supercritical wing for improved supersonic performance, a form of variable-wing camber and canard foreplanes. Trimmed so that the foreplane and wing would be almost equally loaded at high speed, for the lowest possible supersonic drag, the X-29 was drastically unstable at the moment it lifted off the ground, and at all subsonic speeds. One of the major challenges in developing its digital FCS was that any major hardware or software

STOVL performance was judged too risky, and too costly in terms of performance, for the ATF. However, this Lockheed study shows a STOVL multirole supersonic fighter which could be feasible in the late 1990s thanks to improved engine performance. (Lockheed)

failure would cause the aircraft to depart controlled flight so rapidly that the pilot's chance of ejecting safely would be slim. Ultimately, the X-29 emerged with three digital channels so that any two could detect a failure in a third, plus a fourth, analog backup channel which could control the aircraft over a limited flight envelope. The main role of the fourth channel was to protect the aircraft in case some unsuspected freak software or hardware mode disabled all three digital channels simultaneously.

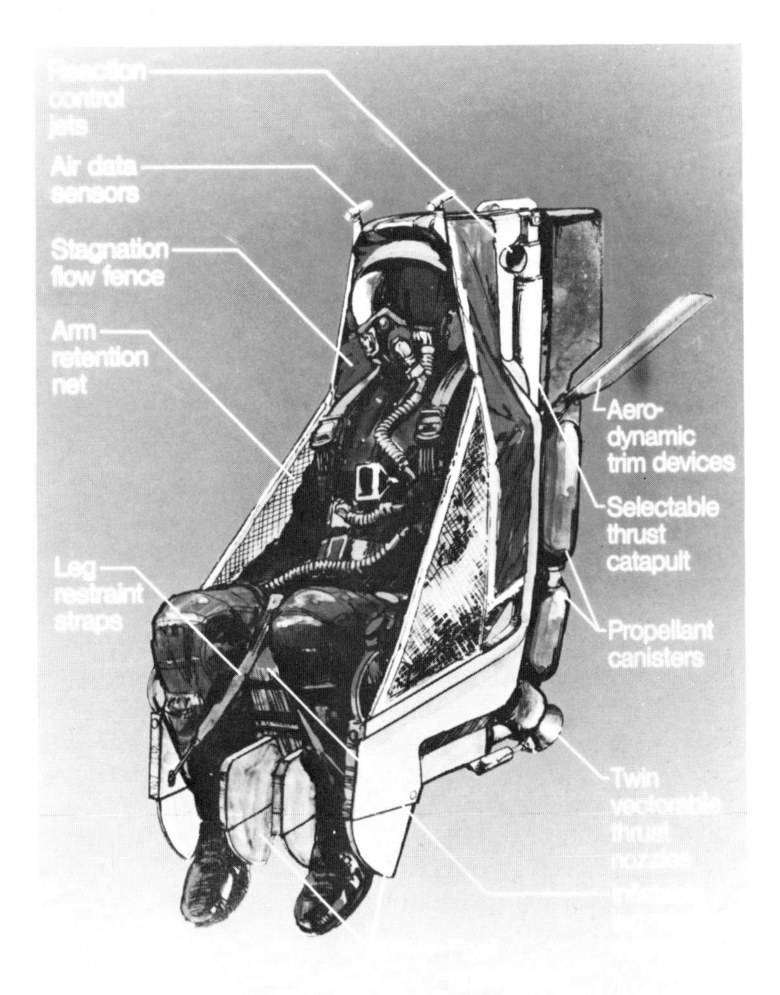

The USAF/Boeing CREST ejection seat is designed to save the pilot's life in extreme conditions which would defeat any current seat. Swiveling motors, control rockets and the variable-thrust catapult are controlled by a computer which constantly monitors the flight conditions and the aircraft's altitude. (Boeing)

As well as featuring FSW and foreplanes, the X-29 was designed with variable-camber flaps on the wing trailing edge—not covered with a smooth, fiberglass skin, like the MAW flaps, but nevertheless designed to create much less drag than conventional flaps—and a pair of strakes extending from the wing trailing edge toward the tail, mainly designed to reduce the risk of a "hung stall" in which the nose would rise so high that not even the canards at full deflection could push it down again. Additional control force was provided by small flaps at the end of the strakes. The X-29 made its first flight in December 1984 at Edwards AFB, and gradually set about expanding the flight envelope and feeding data back to the ATF program.

With the AFTI/F-16, MAW and X-29 programs under way, the USAF's concern was to get flight experience with other important ATF technologies before committing itself to full-scale development of the type. Two of these were firmly identified at the Anaheim meeting October 1982. One was a STOL fighter demonstrator and the other a "supersonic, survivable fighter." In the latter case, "survivable" was largely a euphemism for Stealth, which was so highly classified at the time that people were encouraged not to use the word in public discussions.

The USAF called for proposals on the STOL demonstrator in early 1983, eliciting responses from General Dynamics, based on the F-16, and from McDonnell Douglas, which proposed to modify a two-seat F-15 for the job. The latter won the contract in December 1984, mainly because its F-15 STOL Maneuver Technology Demonstrator (SMTD) offered better performance and could demonstrate more potential STOL techniques than its rival. With only one prototype funded, and an unconventional powerplant, the advantages of having two engines were also significant. The first F-15B two-seater was selected for conversion, and is due to fly in early 1988.

It will look totally unlike any other F-15, because an F-18 stabilizer will have been grafted onto either side of the forward fuselage, immediately in front of the wing. From the rear, the most obvious change will be the replacement of the conventional round exhaust nozzles by oblong, two-dimensional (2-D) nozzles (so called because the nozzle components move in two dimensions rather than three).

Developed by Pratt & Whitney, the 2-D nozzles are complex assemblies of movable panels, valves and cascades. In normal flight, the nozzle opens and closes in the same way as a conventional nozzle. To improve maneuverability, or to rotate the nose upward for a short takeoff, the nozzle can deflect the engine thrust up to thirty degrees upward or downward. To reverse or modulate thrust, the nozzle panels fold inward and forward to block the exhaust stream, which escapes through valves and cascades above and below the exhaust assembly.

Two features distinguish the system from previous thrust reversers; the nozzle can be partly closed, so that part of the thrust is directed aft and part reversed, and the cascades themselves are movable, so that the "reverse" stream can be deflected forward, aft or straight up and down. The forces generated by the shifting of the exhaust stream are very large. The foreplanes help to balance those forces, moving together to provide pitch control and separately to provide roll and yaw inputs.

Developing the nozzle has been a major challenge, but one of the biggest tasks in the F-15 STOL program has been the development of the flight control system. Tra-

This sequence shows how the CREST seat would respond in the case of ejection from a nose-down, inverted position. After the catapult separates the seat from the aircraft, the reaction control jets roll it into an upright but reclined position. Only then do the main rockets fire, canceling the first downward acceleration and lofting the pilot to a safe separation altitude. (Boeing)

A new flight suit, the Tactical Life Support System (TLSS), is being developed by the USAF and Boeing for the ATF and other aircraft. The TLSS integrates many features that have been developed and implemented separately in the past. It combines the functions of a G-suit and pressure suit (the latter is necessary for ATF, because of its high cruising altitude) together with protection against nuclear, biological and chemical (NBC) hazards. The visor is representative of designs which protect the pilot's eyes from laser radiation. (Boeing)

ditionally, flight controls and engine controls have been separate, like the throttle and the stick, but the vectoring and reversing of the nozzle affect the dynamics of the F-15 so drastically that the aircraft would be unflyable if the pilot had to coordinate the operations of the twenty-two devices—cascades, nozzles and aerodynamic control surfaces—that determine the flight path of the aircraft. Instead, the task is carried out by a four-channel digital flight/propulsion control system from General Electric, which receives the pilot's throttle and control demands and implements them according to its own laws. A given stick or throttle movement may have completely different results in different flight phases, but the system is designed to be "transparent" to the pilot; that is, the aircraft responds normally and consistently, and feels like a standard F-15, but can fly more slowly.

Pilots are not the only ones to need NBC protection. Here, two McDonnell Douglas design engineers remove an engine access panel from an F-15 while wearing standard USAF NBC gear. The objective of this exercise was to make the engineers more aware of the conditions under which aircraft may have to be maintained, and encourage them to take these conditions into account in the design of ATF and other future aircraft. (McDonnell Douglas)

The F-15 STOL prototype will also be fitted with the improved radar and head-up display of the F-15E fighter/interdictor, and a FLIR (forward-looking infrared) sensor. The intention is that the pilot should be able to identify the runway using his own radar, and make a precision approach to the point where the FLIR can show the runway on the head-up display. Accurate night landings should then be possible without the aid of electronic beacons on the ground.

The last of the pre-ATF prototype programs, the supersonic demonstrator, did not materialize, mainly because it overlapped the ATF specifications in many respects. Air Force concerns that it would cost too much money, coupled with the manufacturers' fears that the company winning the contract would have an overwhelming advantage in the ATF contest itself, led to its elimination.

While the prototype aircraft programs designed to support the ATF attracted most of the attention, dozens of medium-size contracts and hundreds of smaller ones were issued, covering programs to demonstrate individual technologies needed for the new fighter, from a new hydraulic system and improved power generation to tests in which composite structures were blasted with simulated lightning bolts.

The actual shapes of the ATF contenders are classified, largely because of the Stealth technology used in their design. This USAF artist's impression shows an aircraft not unlike an F-15 in size, but with a modified delta wing and a V-tail. The vertically split, gridded inlets are very unusual. (USAF)

Northrop joined Germany's Dornier company to propose this design, the ND-102, for the Luftwaffe as an alternative to a European aircraft. It has vectoring nozzles instead of a horizontal tail, and a trapezoidal wing. It may be indicative of some features of the Northrop YF-23 ATF competitor. (Northrop)

Boeing's continued work on high-Mach aircraft has resulted in this study for a supersonic interceptor. Like other Boeing concepts, it has a slender wing. Note, also, the large internal weapon bay. (Boeing)

Typical of the larger programs is the USAF/Boeing CREST (Crew Escape Technologies), aimed at producing a new ejection seat for the ATF. CREST is described as an "adaptive" seat. Current ejection seats are effective in many situations but are, essentially, single-mode devices that fire the pilot out of the aircraft with a constant force.

The problems with this approach lie in the fact that there is a compromise between seat performance and seat safety; a greater ejection force will get the pilot out of a crashing aircraft faster, but may cause injury. The CREST seat, however, has an onboard computer linked to the aircraft's own sensors, which constantly monitors altitude, height above ground, airspeed and attitude, and the rates at which all these are changing.

The computer controls a variable-thrust catapult (the explosive device that fires the seat out of the aircraft), variable-thrust sustaining rockets with swiveling nozzles, and a reaction control system. When the pilot starts the ejection sequence, the seat provides the minimum force necessary to clear the aircraft and automatically follows the safest trajectory to ensure a safe separation from the seat.

Grumman proposed an FSW layout for the Advanced Tactical Fighter. Along with Rockwell, however, Grumman was shut out of the fly-off competition and it is unlikely that either of the ATF prototypes has a forward-swept wing. (Grumman)

At high altitude, in level flight and at moderate speed, this may result in a more benign ejection than today's fixed-mode seats, with less risk of injury. But if the aircraft is at low level, in a steep bank and, literally, a split second from ground impact, the seat catapult will fire with maximum force as soon as the canopy starts moving, the vectoring rocket nozzles will rotate the pilot onto his back and the rockets will go to full thrust to lift him to a safe ejection height.

A maximum-force ejection may well injure the pilot, but it is preferable to the alternative. The seat is designed to get the pilot out if ejection is initiated in a thirty-degree dive, with ninety degrees of bank, seventy-five feet off the ground, with three tenths of a second to go. The CREST program started in May 1984 and will result in demonstrations in mid-1988.

By May 1984, a further important step in the definition of the ATF had been taken. Eighteen months earlier, air-to-ground and air-to-air missions had been considered in parallel, but (with the user command enthusiastically pushing all the way) pure air superiority and the replacement of the F-15 became the primary mission. Several factors encouraged the change. Even in 1981 it was increasingly clear that the Soviet Union was moving toward US-style air-superiority fighters and fighter tactics. Developing an aircraft that would be equally capable of air-to-air and air-to-ground missions would be expensive, and raised the ghost of the F-111, a fighter that was designed to do everything and ended up as an overweight and over-budget single-mission aircraft.

Also, McDonnell Douglas and General Dynamics were telling the USAF that the F-15 and F-16 could be adapted into effective long-range strike aircraft. In 1979, McDonnell Douglas borrowed one of the two-seat F-15B development aircraft from the

Rockwell's ATF concept was virtually a flying wing, with a highly blended fuselage and engine nacelles. Control surfaces are mounted between the vectoring engine nozzles. (Rockwell)

USAF and wheeled it into the prototype shop. It went in light gray and came out dark green, festooned with bomb racks and with two massive fuel tanks blended into the fuselage sides. Hughes Aircraft Company added some highly impressive ground-mapping modes to the radar, and a Ford Aerospace Pave Tack pod—a streamlined pannier containing infrared cameras and a laser beam, to guide bombs on to ground targets—was carried on the centerline pylon. But the best feature of the so-called Strike Eagle, in the fighter pilot's view, was that the fuel tanks, sensor pod and bombs could all be removed in a matter of hours at most, leaving an F-15 with an unimpaired ability to kill MiGs.

General Dynamics responded by taking an in-house study for a follow-on F-16 development and adapting it for the strike mission. The changes this time were more than skin deep. The new aircraft, called the F-16XL, had a graphite-skinned "arrow" wing, based on a design originally developed for a supersonic transport. It was al-

It is questionable whether this Lockheed concept bears much relationship to the real YF-22. Configuration and shaping techniques for Stealth are considered highly sensitive, but several features of this design, such as the position of the foreplanes on the body, are highly dubious. (Lockheed)

most two wings in one, with a deep, long-chord inner section, providing ample room for fuel and space for low-drag bomb racks, and a moderately swept, thin-section outer wing for high lift at low speeds. With the new wing and a stretched fuselage, the new F-16 had no less than eighty-two percent more fuel capacity than the standard aircraft, giving it a far greater range. At the same time, the sophisticated wing design was claimed to offer even better maneuvering performance than the standard F-16, together with space for four Sparrow or AMRAAM missiles. Two F-16s were modified into XL prototypes, flying in 1982.

In mid-1983, the USAF decided that a modified F-15 or F-16 would meet its needs for a new air-to-ground fighter, and issued a request for proposals (RFP) – a document setting out what the service required, inviting bids from contractors – on what it called the dual-role fighter (DRF). The RFP was limited to modifications of existing aircraft, limiting the field to the F-16XL and the modified F-15. Unfortunately for General Dynamics, it specified a two-man crew and the use of LANTIRN (low-altitude navigation and targeting by infrared at night), a pair of sophisticated sensor pods, including

A somewhat more believable version of Lockheed's ATF appears to have a wide, shallow ventral inlet and a high degree of blending. However, this picture was issued before the ATF prime contractors were selected. And an element of disinformation – aimed as much at the competition as the GRU – is almost inevitable. (Lockheed)

a radar, infrared imaging equipment and a laser designator, designed to allow a relatively standard fighter to fly precision attack missions at night in overcast weather.

The second seat and LANTIRN were an easier burden for the big F-15 than for the F-16, and General Dynamic's final proposal would probably have needed a more powerful engine to meet the requirement. The F-15 also had the advantage of a much more powerful radar. In February 1984, the Air Force selected the F-15E to meet the DRF requirement. It made its first flight on December 11, 1986, and is due to become operational in early 1989.

With the dual-role fighter program under way, and the ATF directed toward the air-to-air mission, the USAF could close in on a definitive specification for the new fighter. Throughout 1984, in constant touch with the industry, the ATF program office, under Colonel Albert C. Piccirillo, boiled down the service's many requirements and desires to produce a specification that could be met at a reasonable cost. The task was long, detailed and painstaking. Every pound of equipment added to the aircraft meant a five-pound increase in gross weight to meet the same performance requirements. "Early in this stage," Piccirillo said a few months later, "we found four or five significant drivers"—these were specific requirements which added a great deal to the fighter's weight—"and making just one of them cost us 10,000 pounds." In other cases, Piccirillo said, "backing off by half a percent was important."

After four complete drafts, the Air Force reached a near-final requirement at the end of 1984, calling for an air-to-air fighter to replace the F-15. It would have greater range, with an operational radius of about 800 miles; it would be able to cruise at Mach 1.4 or more as long as it was operating over hostile territory, and it would be able to maneuver at 6 g up to Mach 1.8.

The USAF also imposed weight and cost limits. The service felt that the aircraft need weigh no more than an F-15C, when the two were loaded for a normal air-superiority mission. The F-15C, which is heavier than the original F-15A, weighs about 50,000 pounds with eight missiles, ammunition and an external fuel tank.

For the first time, the USAF published its cost targets for a new aircraft before issuing the RFP; the ATF was to cost no more than $40 million per copy in 1985 dollars, once production was in full swing. The question of cost was looming in importance, because each generation of tactical aircraft was tending to cost far more than the one before it. Norman Augustine, president of Martin-Marietta, had extrapolated the trend to 2054 and concluded that, in that year, the entire US defense budget would suffice for one tactical fighter, which would be operated by the Navy on odd-numbered days and by the Air Force on even-numbered days. Realistic or not, Augustine's projections showed that costs had run out of control, and the Air Force knew that costs had at least to be capped. The ATF would cost more to buy than an F-15, but the increase was nothing as dramatic as the cost difference between an F-15 and an F-4.

The USAF also set limits on the total "life-cycle cost" (LCC) of the ATF. LCC was a concept originated by Northrop in the 1950s, and includes not only the cost of the aircraft but all its operating costs from its first flight to the day it is retired from its primary mission. LCC includes fuel, oil and spares, and the cost of training, housing, transporting and paying the people who operate the aircraft. While nobody pretends that LCC can be predicted to the dollar, the computer models used to calculate it have been refined to the point where comparisons between aircraft designed for similar missions can be quite accurate. In the case of the ATF, the LCC was to be no higher than that of the F-15.

The structure of the development program was also novel. The USAF had run into problems with the traditional approach, where a single contractor was selected to develop the aircraft. In a number of programs in the 1970s, the USAF had ordered low-cost, sparsely equipped prototypes from two companies and had flown them before making its final choice. "Fly-before-buy," however, had disadvantages for ATF. For one thing, the aircraft was ambitious and would cost a great deal to develop, and building competing prototypes would be expensive. Another factor was that electronics would be very important to ATF, and test-flying a couple of bare-bones proto-

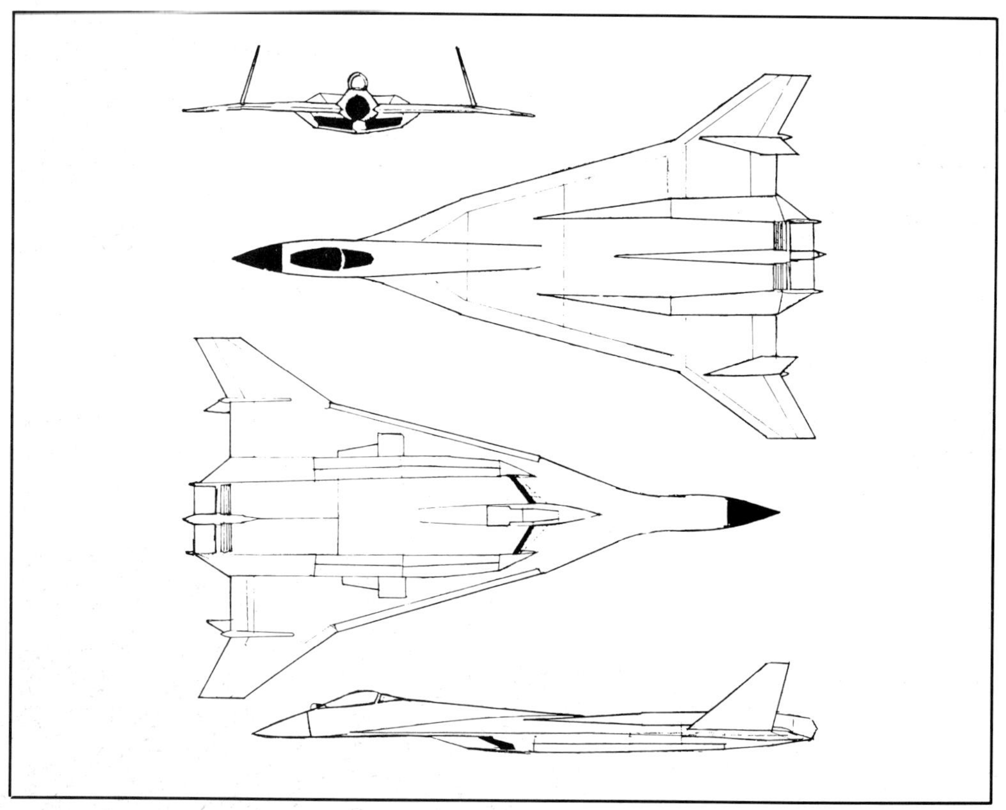

Author's impression of a possible ATF layout, using a slender arrow wing with vortex flaps and thrust vectoring to handle the maneuvering requirement. Missile bays are located outboard of the engines, and all surfaces are angled away from the vertical to minimize radar cross-section.

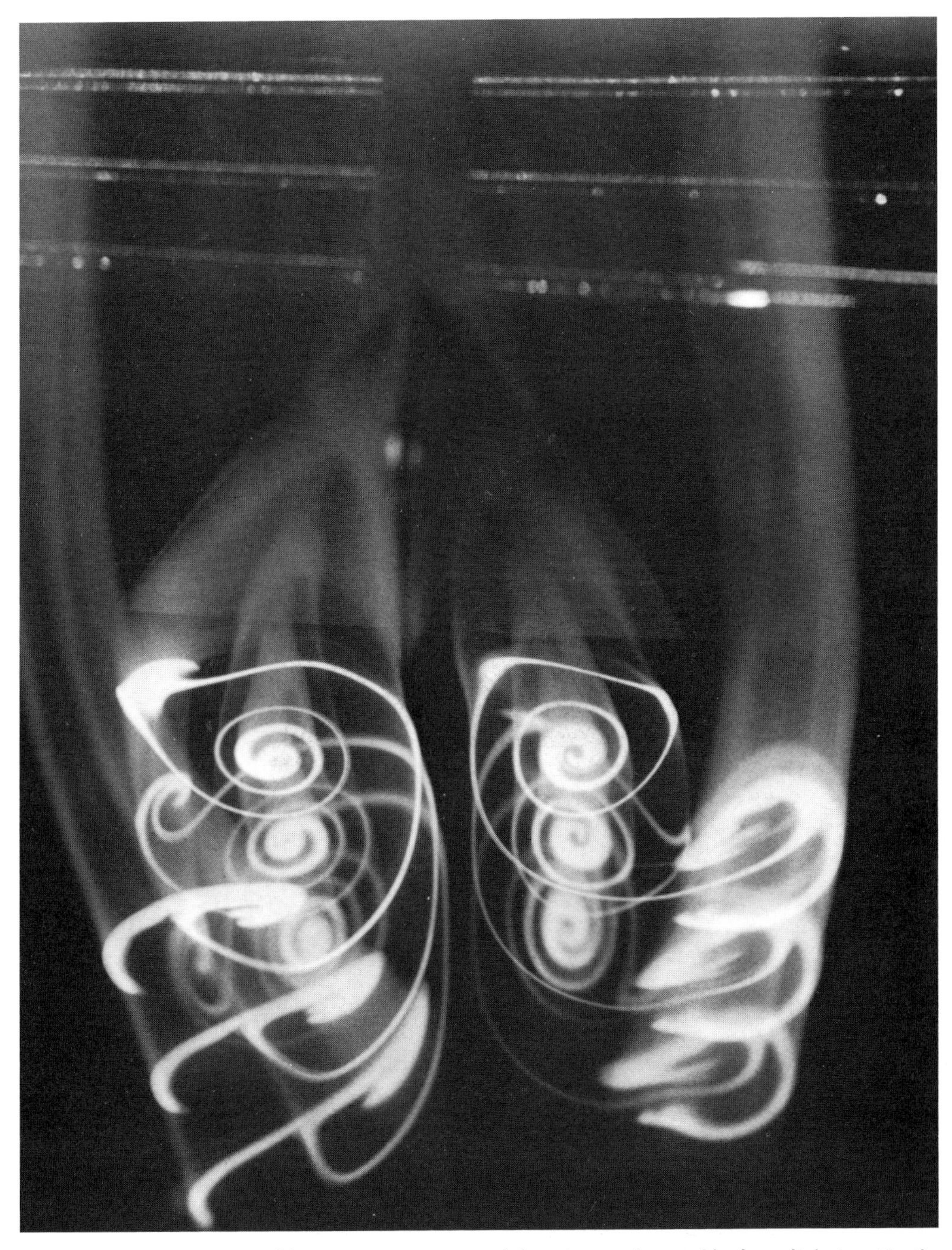

Vortex patterns over a delta wing are imaged by laser light in a Northrop demonstration. (Northrop)

type aircraft would tell the service little about this crucial area. Also, the Air Force could not afford to fly more than two prototypes, and this could lead to a painful and difficult decision if three or four of the proposals turned out to be of similar quality.

The solution was to develop the ATF through a competitive "demonstration/validation" (Dem-Val) phase, which would encompass almost everything except flight testing. During Dem-Val, the contractors would build and test simulated cockpits and complete avionics systems, and would build mock-ups to prove that their aircraft would meet USAF targets for reduced maintenance. Other full-scale models would be used to demonstrate the design's reduced radar signature, while extensive wind-tunnel testing would be carried out to prove and refine the external design.

The USAF was in a strong position to impose cost ceilings, because by 1984 ATF was the only new fighter program in sight. The Navy's proposed multirole fighter, VFMX, had been abandoned, and the Europeans were less interested than usual in transatlantic collaboration. If the US manufacturers did not like the USAF's numbers, their only option was to get out of the fighter business.

All the possible candidates responded to the USAF's RFP for the Advanced Tactical Fighter, issued in September 1985, even though the target price had been cut to $35 million by the Pentagon. Seven companies submitted proposals, each comprising thousands of pages of computer printouts and charts, weighing tons in all. (In an

During the first round of the ATF competition, in 1985, Boeing built a complete wing for its ATF design from thermoplastic/graphite composite material. This is one of the skins, formed in one piece. (Boeing)

earlier competition, one company chartered a freighter to deliver its proposal to Wright-Patterson.)

Of the seven competitors, General Dynamics and McDonnell Douglas seemed to have a head start, as the producers of virtually all the USAF's supersonic fighters since the early 1960s. Grumman, the other US company established as a prime contractor for complex fighters, had built the F-14, but had never built an Air Force fighter in quantity. Northrop had seemed to be an underdog in the US fighter business, producing thousands of low-cost F-5 fighters for export but never winning the big fighter contracts. When a Northrop basic design was accepted by the Navy—the F-18—McDonnell Douglas took over as prime contractor. Lockheed, similarly, was a technologically powerful company, but was regarded as a developer of exotic, specialized and expensive aircraft rather than workaday tactical fighters. Rockwell was so heavily preoccupied with B-1 work that its ability to respond to the RFP was limited. And lastly, Boeing seemed to be the ultimate outsider at first glance; the company had never built a jet fighter or a supersonic aircraft, and had not flown a new combat aircraft since 1952. However, Boeing's expertise in making complex electronic systems work together, as demonstrated on the navigation and bombing systems of the B-52 and B-1, and its skill in efficient production techniques gave it more of a chance than most people might have thought.

The outcome was not quite what most people expected, for a reason that could be summed up in one word: Stealth. As the definition of the ATF continued, the production version of Lockheed's secret Stealth fighter started operational testing above Nellis AFB and other Western test ranges. Its success in confounding simulated Soviet SAM radars appears to have eliminated a great deal of the skepticism toward Stealth that had existed in the early 1980s. Even after the RFP was issued, the USAF pushed to get as much Stealth as possible into the ATF.

In January 1986, the service announced that the deadline for replies would be extended to late April, so the contractors could carry out more work on Stealth technology. When the USAF evaluated the seven final responses, two of them stood out above all the others; they were from Lockheed and Northrop, the two companies that had worked longest and hardest on Stealth, and which were responsible for the first two operational Stealth aircraft.

The fact that two of the ATF proposals were clearly superior to the others meshed neatly with the recommendations of the Packard Commission—led by electronics pioneer and industrialist David Packard—which had been convened in 1984 to reexamine Pentagon procurement techniques. Its report had strongly favored building and flying competing prototypes.

In May 1986, Secretary of the Air Force Edward C. Aldridge announced that the USAF would order flying prototypes of two ATF designs. The decision was partly political, to show that the USAF was prepared to accept outside advice. As noted, the USAF had exhaustively evaluated the pros and cons of a "fly-off" before settling on the Dem-Val program, but the fact that the Lockheed and Northrop proposals led the pack made the decision easier to take. It was also felt that the designers could emphasize Stealth to a greater extent in the prototype aircraft, knowing that they would be flying six years before service entry and that there would be time to fix most problems that might emerge.

About the same time, a further significant change in the program was announced. Under pressure to coordinate their plans better, the USAF and US Navy agreed to cooperate on their main tactical combat aircraft programs. The US Navy is working on a long-range, heavy-payload Stealth bomber, called the Advanced Tactical Aircraft or ATA. Little is known of this aircraft, beyond the fact that Northrop and Grumman, and McDonnell Douglas and General Dynamics, are working on a Dem-Val program.

Under the joint agreement, the USAF would consider ATA for its future strike requirements, while the Navy would regard the ATF as the logical successor to the F-14. The hook buried in the agreement was that each service's requirements would be considered in the other's program. In the case of the ATA, this would have no great impact, but the ATF might have to be designed so that a carrier-based version could be developed without a major rework. One manufacturer's response was to send a

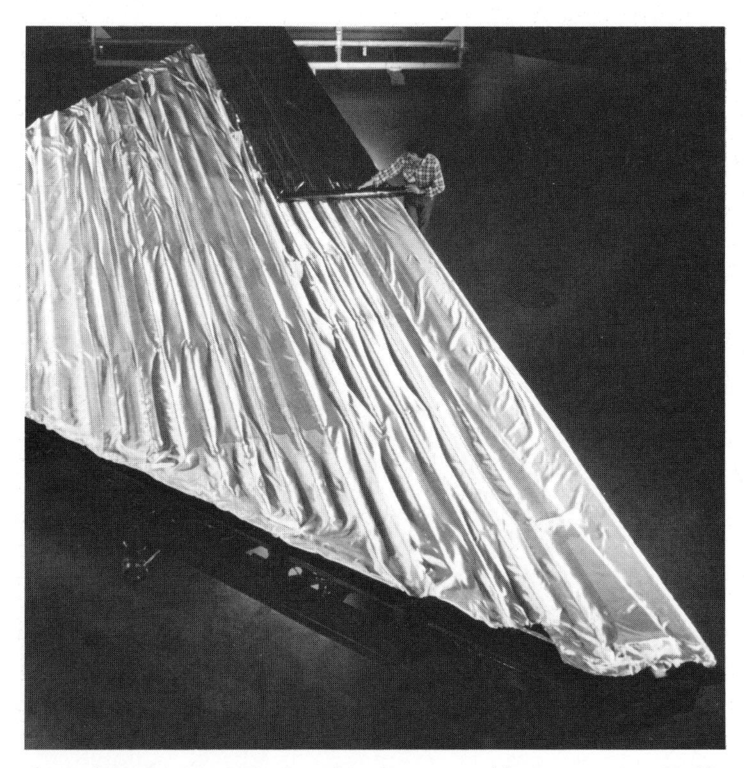

One of the Boeing ATF wing skins is prepared for processing. Unlike conventional epoxy-based composites, thermoplastic components do not have to be cured simultaneously under heat and pressure, so very large pieces can be formed without using an enormous autoclave. (Boeing)

videotape of hard carrier landings to the ATF program office; the message was that the USAF/USN agreement had made weight and cost targets that much harder to attain.

The final step in the shaping of the ATF program came in the summer of 1986. First, General Dynamics, Lockheed and Boeing announced an agreement under which they would team to develop the ATF if one of their proposals was selected. A couple of weeks later, McDonnell Douglas and Northrop announced a similar arrangement. The final decision was, as usual, announced on a Friday afternoon, after the stock markets had closed. Air Force Secretary Aldridge chose Los Angeles as the place to announce Southern California's victory: Lockheed and Northrop were selected to build two prototype aircraft each, with the first flight set for 1989.

By the spring of 1987, no drawings or mock-up photographs of either the Northrop YF-23 or the Lockheed YF-22 had been released, mainly because the shapes of

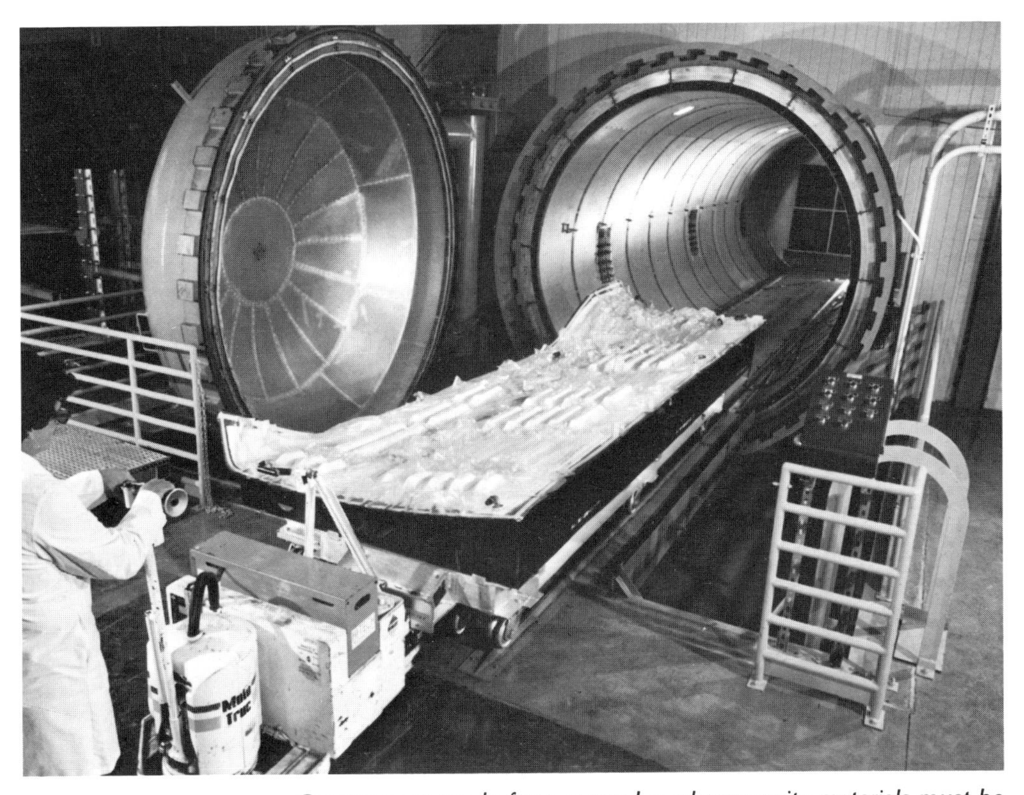

Components made from epoxy-based composite materials must be "cured" in an autoclave, under heat and pressure. The curing process is irreversible, so that any faulty component must be scrapped. Thermoplastic-based materials, however, can be reheated and remolded. (Boeing)

both aircraft include unconventional features designed to reduce their radar cross section (RCS). These will be far more apparent than they are on the European canards, because the ATF is intended to be much more Stealthy than these aircraft. European planners are settling for a reduction of around fifty percent in the head-on RCS of their new fighters, when measured in the X-band used by most fighter radars. This is not hard to attain, using common sense and some radar-absorbent material (RAM) in critical areas. ATF, however, is intended to use Stealth as protection against fighters, SAM radars and Mainstay AEW&C aircraft, all of them operating in different wave bands. The USAF's goal is to reduce its all-around RCS by a factor of 100, compared to the F-15.

Stealth has a fundamental effect on aircraft shape, and while no recent Stealth design has been depicted in any unclassified drawing, it can be said that such aircraft are strange or even bizarre in appearance. Accustomed as we are to shapes determined by trades between mission requirements and the laws of aerodynamics, we are likely to be surprised at the appearance of an aircraft designed largely according to the laws of electromagnetic wave propagation.

For example, it is possible that the external shape could be composed of flat panels, all carefully angled in different directions and none large enough to generate a strong main-beam reflection. It is also likely that the engine inlets would be very unconventional, differing from current design practice as much as later supersonic inlets differed from subsonic designs. The reader is advised to put himself or herself inside the head of an observer to whom the F-86 Sabre represents the state of the art, and to imagine this observer's reaction to the sight of an A-5 Vigilante.

Another way in which the ATF will differ from contemporary fighters is that it will usually be free from the clutter of fuel tanks, missiles and pylons that festoon the F-16 or F-15 in service. The reason is that such features are hard to reconcile with supersonic cruise, and are out of the question if Stealth is the objective.

Providing an internal weapons bay in a fighter, in particular, is a triple challenge. First, inserting large open cavities in a densely packed structure stressed to 9 g is difficult. Second, studies have consistently shown that fighters and tactical bombers are better off with external weapons, because the extra drag of the weapon on the outbound trip is more than offset by the fact that the airplane itself can be smaller, lighter and cheaper without the extra volume of the weapons bay inside. Third, how do you launch a missile quickly, reliably and safely from an internal bay at Mach 1.8 and 6 g?

On the other hand, we know or can guess a few things about the shape of the YF-22 and YF-23. As noted earlier, in clean condition they will weigh about as much as the F-15C with its 600-US-gallon external tank. They will have about the same wingspan but will probably be a few feet longer, to accommodate more internal fuel. Greater use of wing-to-body blending, as practiced on the SR-71, F-16 and B-1, is an effective way of providing more internal volume for fuel and weapons without much more drag, and will be very apparent on the ATF.

Modern technology provides the designer with a wider selection of basic wing planforms than was available in the 1970s. At one end of the spectrum, new materials, aeroelastic tailoring and MAW technology make it possible to design long-span, relatively slender wings—which are efficient in all flight regimes—with the very thin sections essential for low transonic and supersonic drag. One McDonnell Douglas design study, dating from 1981, featured a completely unswept wing with a thickness-to-chord ratio of only three percent—meaning it would have been less than two inches thick at the root.

A completely opposite approach to wing design has been studied by the National Aeronautics and Space Administration (NASA) and some fighter manufacturers, including Northrop. Rather than tackling the structural problems of slender wings, this approach emphasizes making highly swept or delta wings more efficient, particularly at low speeds and high angles of attack, by exploiting a characteristic of such wings, which was observed in the 1950s. On a moderately swept or straight wing, the airflow over the wing breaks down completely as the angle of the wing to the air passes a certain point. On a sharply swept leading edge, however, the airflow tends to form a stable helical pattern, or vortex, looking like a small tornado.

Knowing that this phenomenon existed, however, was not the same as knowing how or why it happened or how to make best use of it. In the 1950s and 1960s, vortex

Full-scale models of the YF-22 and YF-23 ATF prototypes will be tested on outdoor radar ranges such as this one, operated by Martin Marietta Corporation, to evaluate the Stealth features of their design. What appears to be a runway is an almost perfectly flat surface, with an illuminating radar at one end and a radar-absorbent pylon, on which the test specimen is mounted, at the other. (Martin Marietta)

flows were exploited in a number of ways, usually to stabilize airflows over swept or delta wings. The Anglo-French Concorde supersonic airliner and the SR-71 both rely on vortices in low-speed flight to reduce landing and takeoff speeds. The F-16 and F-18 both use vortices shed by their leading-edge root extensions (LERXs) to stabilize the airflow over their wings and vertical stabilizers in high-speed maneuvers. However, even at the time the F-16XL was designed, chief project engineer Harry Hillaker described vortex flow as "a black art" rather than an exact science; the design of the F-18's complex LERXs had consumed thousands of hours of wind-tunnel time, and dozens of costly models had been built and modified to evaluate different shapes.

Another tool for radar-cheating design is the indoor subscale test facility, such as this chamber at LTV's plant near Dallas. The room is lined with carbon-treated foam pyramids, which absorb radar with great efficiency. (LTV)

Since then, however, designers have been using new tools to predict and map vortex flows. One of these is the supercomputer. The extremely powerful devices now being developed have speeds in the realm of billions of floating-point operations per second (in computerese, gigaflops) and are reaching the point where they can calculate the trajectory of each molecule of air around a body, according to complex equations that take account of compressibility and turbulence. The first numerical aerodynamic simulator (NAS) aimed at this capability is now being put into service at NASA's Ames Research Center, south of San Francisco, and similar systems are being developed by major manufacturers.

The advantages of such "computer wind tunnels" are great. They are not subject to scale effects or to physical limits on airspeed and model size. Dynamic effects—such as the change in airflow as an aircraft pitches upward under aerodynamic loads—can be simulated in real time, rather than being reconstructed from a series of tests on a fixed model. Design changes can be implemented almost instantly, and their exact effects can be observed and quantified as they happen instead of being deduced by changed forces in the model. The hope is that tough design problems that have resisted solution by conventional means, including some of the mysteries of vortex flow, can be beaten with the NAS.

A less esoteric but still useful tool for aerodynamicists, particularly in the study of vortex flows, is the scanning laser beam. Reflective particles are released into the wind tunnel, and a laser is used to illuminate a very thin slice of the space around the model. This can be filmed or photographed, giving the aerodynamicist a very clear picture of the vortex flow at that point.

Increasing knowledge of vortex flows has led to the discovery that a properly designed leading-edge flap can control and contain the vortex, in turn helping the flow over the rest of the wing to remain stable. While the flap would normally be expected to produce drag, the vortex itself can generate suction on the flap surface, providing lift and thrust.

With vortex lift, the ATF could have a deceptively simple wing planform, surprisingly like that of an F-106. Again, the ATF wing could combine the two thrusts in aerodynamics in the form of an "arrow" wing, with a deep, highly swept section inboard, blended into the fuselage, and a thin, less-swept outboard section mounting high-lift flaps.

Most impressions of ATF studies have shown aircraft without conventional horizontal tails. Whether the F-22 or F-23 will have a canard configuration, however, is a moot point, perhaps surprisingly in view of the canard's popularity in Europe. It can be argued that the combination of MAW, vectored thrust and vortex lift can generate enough maneuvering force to make the canard unnecessary, eliminating its weight, its drag and its contribution to RCS, and leaving a completely tailless configuration, like the F-16XL or some Northrop designs. On the other hand, the canard may be needed in order to improve STOL performance.

Stealth considerations may well rule out the single vertical stabilizer, as used on the EFA; the shape is a strong natural reflector from the beam aspect, and the surface is thin, complicating the use of absorbent material. Twin, sharply angled fins are likely, and could be set out on the wingtips if the wings are far enough aft. One McDonnell Douglas study shows such a layout. Alternatively, fins could be located on the rear fuselage, and angled outward enough to provide a measure of pitch control, like the V-tail on a Beech Bonanza.

What *is* certain is that the control surfaces and vectoring nozzles on the ATF will be working together under the control of powerful computers to give the pilot the impression that he is flying an entirely straightforward, simple airplane; the actual aircraft will be so complex, and will have so many flight modes, that the pilot would not be able to exploit them all. Instead, the pilot will issue a command and the system will interpret it. For instance, if the pilot pulls back sharply on the stick, the control system will first deflect the vectoring nozzles upward, and the MAW flaps downward, to rotate the fuselage and start the aircraft into the maneuver. As the aircraft begins to change course and g-forces increase, the outboard MAW flaps will move up again, to reduce the loads on the wing structure; the nozzles will return to their normal position for maximum thrust. If the pilot leaves the stick in the same position,

There is some concern that lightning or nuclear flash could damage composite or radar-absorbent material (RAM), or render some types of RAM less effective. In this test, a prototype composite-fuselage helicopter (a Bell D292, developed under an Army program) is subjected to a powerful electromagnetic discharge. (Boeing)

the flaps and nozzles will set themselves for minimum drag. The entire process will be automatic.

The ATF's structure will not be conventional, largely because of the dictates of Stealth. While careful shaping can reduce RCS to some extent, what can be achieved by configuration alone is not very significant in tactical terms. What makes the difference is RAM, or radar-absorbent material. RAM was first developed during World War II, to protect the snorkels and conning towers of German submarines from the search radars fitted to Allied reconnaissance aircraft, and since then has been steadily improved.

The critical considerations in evaluating RAM include the degree to which it suppresses the radar echo, usually measured in decibels: the degree to which its absorption performance varies according to the angle from which the radar wave arrives, and the radar's wavelength; and the material's bulk, weight and strength.

From unclassified sources, it appears that there are two main categories of RAM: dielectric and magnetic. The common principle of both these RAM types is that their active ingredient is a material with many free electrons in its molecular structure; this material may be nonconductive (dielectric), such as carbon, or magnetic, such as ferrite. When an electromagnetic wave impinges on such a material, the free electrons align themselves with the wave. Radar pulses, however, are based on high-frequency sine waves, which cause the electrons to realign themselves at the same rate. This process is not 100 percent efficient, and the effect is that some of the radar energy is retained as heat.

High-performance RAM of either kind is usually designed so that the quantity of the active ingredient increases gradually from the front to the back of the material. The reason for this is that all absorbers soak up part of the wave and reflect the rest. In a layered, graduated RAM, the front face is lightly loaded with absorber and mainly transparent to radar. As the wave penetrates the material, absorption and reflection gradually increase, but the reflected waves must make their way back out through the absorber. Once again, part of the wave is absorbed, and part is reflected back into the RAM.

Magnetic RAM is generally considered to offer greater absorption per unit of thickness than dielectric RAM, but it is also quite heavy. In its commonest form, it consists of an active absorber in a polymer base and is like a thick, rather heavy rubber sheet; it is designed to be bonded to a conductive metal skin. However, the British Plessey company also has a new product known as ADRAM (advanced dielectric RAM), which appears to be as thin and flexible as the magnetic RAM but is very much lighter. However, these types of RAM are all "parasitic," contributing nothing to the strength of the aircraft structure, and are difficult to use on a highly loaded fighter airframe except in small quantities.

One solution to this problem is radar-absorbent structure (RAS), using the same electromagnetic principles as RAM but made in the form of honeycomb panels. A honeycomb has an internal core made from a flexible synthetic material (DuPont's Nomex is most commonly used), formed into small hexagonal chambers, so that it is very resistant to crushing stresses. This core is bonded to inner and outer skins of graphite or other high-strength composite materials to create light, rigid load-bearing panels.

Honeycomb RAS is made in the same way, but the outer skin is made from a composite that is virtually transparent to radar—such as DuPont's Kevlar—and the core is treated with an absorber, so that the density of the active ingredient is increased from front to back. Such material has been developed for the Northrop Advanced Technology Bomber, the so-called Stealth bomber, which is due to fly in early 1988.

Composites are not the only new material technology that could find a place on ATF. Here, an F-15 component is being formed by superplastic forming/diffusion bonding of titanium. Alloy sheets are heated to a very high temperature, until they become soft, and are "blown" into shape by inert gas. By using multiple sheets, it is possible to produce quite complex components quickly, with very little material wastage. (McDonnell Douglas)

The trouble with RAS, as the foregoing description might suggest, is that it is extremely expensive. The material itself has to be made very precisely in order to sustain the desired absorbing effect. A Stealthy aircraft must also be assembled with great precision, because even the smallest gaps in the structure can cause radar reflections large enough to negate the effects of RAS. In order to meet the cost targets for the ATF, some changes are likely in materials and manufacturing.

The main change in materials will be the introduction of new composite materials based on thermoplastic resins. Briefly, the epoxy resins used in the past to bind glass, carbon or aramid fibers together are "thermosetting" plastics; once they are formed under heat and pressure, their molecular structure changes irreversibly. Thermoplastics, by contrast, can be reheated and re-formed.

Talking about thermoplastics, one company's ATF program manager said he had been accused of trying to build an airplane from Tupperware. The new composite materials combine high-strength fibers such as graphite with newly developed plastics such as polyether-ether-ketone (PEEK) and polyphenylene sulfide (PPS). These plastics are tougher than those of ten years ago, and more resistant to heat and chemicals. New thermoplastics with even higher temperature limits are being developed for applications such as the ATF.

For the aerospace manufacturer, the most important advantage of thermoplastic composite material is the lower cost of the finished part. To begin with, thermoplastics do not have to be stored in refrigerators, unlike thermosets. Rather than being cured during fabrication, thermoplastic composites are formed by the same processes used for injection molding. Molding is not only faster than curing, but also makes it possible to create a larger variety of complex shapes. Another convenient attribute of thermoplastic composite parts is that they can be bonded with a wide variety of adhesives. Also very important is the fact that a flawed thermoplastic composite part can be repaired and remolded; a thermoset part with even a minor flaw is rubbish, unusable even for scrap.

Because of all these factors, the cost of a thermoplastic composite component can be forty to fifty percent lower than an equivalent thermoset component. In most other respects, too, thermoplastics are equivalent or superior to thermosets. In particular, the thermoplastic resins are much tougher and less likely to be damaged by impact; they are less susceptible to attack from moisture, fuel and other chemicals; and they are very resistant to fire.

In view of the widespread use of new materials and the tough cost restrictions, the ATF program should benefit greatly from the USAF's efforts to improve the manufacturing technology used by the aerospace industry. Aircraft manufacture has always been labor-intensive—"airplanes are built of manhours," one production expert has said—but the increasing complexity of modern aircraft, and traditions of manual assembly and hand-fitting, has made production costs even more important.

Most of today's aircraft factories follow patterns laid down in World War II. The airplane takes shape as it moves down the production line, and workers swarm over it at each station, riveting and fastening parts into place. Although the machine tools that form some basic parts of the aircraft are computer-controlled, most of the work is done by hand, and most of the single parts are small. After the structure is finished, the many lines, wires and hoses are installed, followed by the electronics. Huge and expensive inventories of the myriad small parts of the aircraft are maintained in storage areas adjacent to the production line, held in numbered racks. A worker who needs a part has to consult a large-scale blueprint of the area in question, find the part number and obtain it from the store. The fundamental problem is that most of these plants are leased from the government, and up to now nobody has bothered to make the investment necessary to re-equip them.

The ATF production line, as it approaches its maximum rate in 1994, should look very different. It will make much greater use of computers. Since the F-15 and F-16

Building a combat aircraft by the means used today is labor-intensive and often costly. This view of a Grumman A-6F undergoing electrical testing illustrates some of the problems. The ATF, which will rely more on avionics than any current fighter, will require innovations in manufacturing. (Grumman)

were designed, most manufacturers have made a wholesale shift to CAD (computer-aided design), which relates to the traditional drawing board as a word processor relates to a typewriter.

The first CAD workstations allowed the designer to make conventional drawings on a computer screen. Later systems allowed the operator to view the part in perspective, from any angle, to rotate it and to move one part relative to another. An example of the early benefits of CAD is the F-18's main landing gear, which has a "knee"

This Lockheed impression shows ATF production in a "factory of the future." Advanced handling devices are used to lift complete aircraft so that robots can install components in the underside of the fuselage. Parts are delivered by automated vehicles. The entire aircraft exists as a single computer database, accessible from control points on the assembly floor. (Lockheed)

joint allowing it to fold into a compact space, clear the fuselage-mounted Sparrow missiles, and still have a wide track for stability. The apparently complex retraction involves only one swiveling joint and one actuator, but the precise relationship of the joint axis, the trunnion and the actuator could not have been defined without CAD.

CAD not only improves the design product, but as the aircraft is designed it takes shape not only as drawings and printouts but also as an electronic database. This, for example, gives the individual engineer the ability to overlay all the system runs, separately or together, on the part that he or she is designing. On new aircraft, manufacturers are striving for a new level of completeness in the database, so that, for example, literally every hole and attachment point is on the structural drawing as soon as it is released.

The next step is CAD/CAM (computer-aided design/computer-aided manufacture), in which production tools and machine instructions are made directly from the database. This has already been shown to result in better-fitting parts and reduced assembly time. Also, the database can be made accessible to the assembly-line worker, through shop-floor terminals, so that parts can be rapidly identified and ordered electronically. Still identified by the same computer code, they can be automatically picked from the store and ferried to the workplace aboard robotic carts.

The physical assembly of the ATF will also be different. Honeycomb, for example, lends itself to the use of large, one-piece panels; unlike conventional structure, honeycomb panels are inherently stiff and do not have to be supported by ribs every few inches. Instead of aligning dozens of ribs and frames in complex tools, the ATF assembly-line workers may put together a much simpler skeleton, and bond a few large sections—resembling parts of a full-size hobby model—to the frames.

The installation of the many internal components can be helped by fitting them before major assembly takes place, if possible, so that workers have more room to move around them. Other components, such as electronics and cockpit instruments, may be assembled outside the aircraft on thermoplastic composite subframes and pretested before being placed in the aircraft.

The challenge facing the ATF's developers is to use one group of advanced technologies—in computing, materials and manufacturing—to make another group affordable, and to slow down the steadily rising trend in aircraft costs. Limiting the airframe costs is vital because, for the first time in a tactical fighter, only a minority of the aircraft's total flyaway cost is allocated for airframe and systems. In the ATF program, propulsion, avionics and weapons will be emphasized as never before.

Chapter 4

Power for the new fighters

Look closely at any high-technology fighter engine, and the first thing that is apparent is that it is put together like a one-and-a-half-ton Swiss watch. Even the biggest parts are precisely machined; every bolt, fastener and pin is of the highest quality, and everything fits to tolerances measured in thousandths of an inch.

The engine is made that way because it must be. In the back of a modern jet engine, gas temperatures run well above the melting point of any known metal. Turbine wheels, feet in diameter, spin at speeds of 10,000 revolutions per minute, and the centrifugal loads are so enormous that, if the disk fails, blades and bits of metal will be flung straight through the engine carcass and into the airframe with the force of cannon shells. Each of the high-pressure turbine blades, barely bigger than one's thumb, must extract 400 horsepower from the gas stream to spin the compressor. No wonder engine development has proven to be the toughest part of many fighter programs, or that so many engine designers have gray hair.

Pushing the limits of engine technology is necessary, however, because the engine has an enormous impact on the performance of the aircraft, both because of its own weight and the fact that it consumes fuel. If the weight of the engine can be reduced by ten percent for the same thrust, and the specific fuel consumption (SFC), or the fuel burn per unit of power, can also be cut by the same amount, the entire aircraft can be ten percent smaller for the same mission. At the extreme corners of the flight envelope, such as sustained maneuvers at high g, the weight of the engine may actually be critical to meeting requirements at all.

"All the good things in engine design come from high pressure ratio," an engineer once told me, "and so do all the bad things." Pressure ratio, like compression ratio on an automobile engine, is the ratio of the maximum pressure inside the engine to the pressure of the air in the inlet. High pressure ratio means that the engine can do more work with the same volume of air, so that it can generate more thrust for its size and weight.

It also improves thermal efficiency; there is less air, so a greater proportion of it is used in combustion rather than just being pumped through the engine and soaking up heat. The result is that high-pressure engines are more efficient. However, high pressures go hand in hand with high temperatures at the rear of the engine. Also, high-pressure air finds leaks (around the turbine roots and tips, for example) where low-pressure air will not pass, so that the engine will not perform at its greatest efficiency.

Another phenomenon associated with high pressure ratios is stalling or surging, analogous to a wing stalling, in which the airflow through the blades breaks down and the engine refuses to swallow air. Stalls are particularly likely to happen when the throttle is "slammed" fully open at low speeds and high angles of attack, as may often happen during a dogfight.

Since the first fighter jet engines appeared, thrust/weight ratio has steadily increased. The first J57 produced about three pounds of thrust for every pound of weight; the improved J75 was up to 4:1, and the J79 was just below 5:1. The TF30, in the early 1960s, set a standard at 6:1. However, when the USAF wanted an aircraft that could outturn and outmaneuver subsonic fighters, with their light weight and large wings, while retaining the speed and climb capability to intercept the MiG-25 Foxbat, the requirement arose for an engine developing eight pounds of thrust for each pound of weight. This engine became the Pratt & Whitney F100, which powers the F-15 and the majority of F-16s.

The F100 set the performance standard for later fighter engines, but not even its greatest fans would argue that its development was easy. The engine suffered from two specific, severe problems—stalls and turbine failures—and was in some respects difficult to maintain. The experience is worth discussing, because the lessons of the F100 have affected every subsequent fighter engine program, and many of the

A Pratt & Whitney F100-PW-229 unleashes its full 29,000 pounds of thrust during a ground test, more than eight pounds of thrust for every pound of weight. (Pratt & Whitney)

features introduced as the engine was fixed will be standard for next-generation powerplants.

The worst of the F100's stall problem was that the engine suffered from "stagnation stalls" in which airflow through the engine stopped completely and, often, could not be restarted without slowing the engine virtually to idle speed. Many of these stalls were eventually traced to the augmentor, at the back of the engine. The F100 is an augmented bypass engine, in which almost half the air that enters the engine leaves it before reaching the high-pressure compressor and passes down a duct surrounding the rest of the engine.

The augmentor is a burner, located aft of the primary exhaust, in which the oxygen-rich flow from the bypass duct and the engine core is mixed with fuel and ignited to produce a thrust increase of some seventy percent for takeoff and combat. It was found, however, that the control system that fed fuel to the augmentor lost precision as the engine grew older, so that the pressure in the augmentor would fluctuate or "spike" as much as twenty percent above or below the design level. The pressure wave would propagate back up the engine and stall the fan.

Another major problem, premature turbine failures, stemmed paradoxically from the engine's excellent thrust/weight ratio. Older fighters had less power, so their pilots usually left the throttle wide open during combat. Because F-15 and F-16 pilots had so much more power to play with, they played hard, slamming the throttle forward and backward during mock engagements. The problem was that the designers of the F100 had used the life cycles of older engines as the model for the new engine

Typical of modern fighter engines, the General Electric F404 powers the US Navy's F-18, the Gripen and the X-29. The engine produces almost eight pounds of thrust per pound of weight. (General Electric)

and had assumed, as had been the case when earlier engines had been developed, that the usual endurance tests would reveal any problems. Once the F100 reached the hands of operational pilots, it was found that the engine was going from low to high operating temperatures and back again far more often than anyone had expected, and the result was failures and excessive wear.

Another effect of the unexpectedly hard use to which the engine was being put was that it needed frequent "trimming" to maintain power. All jet engines have an automatic control system to regulate fuel flow to the combustors, and to govern the movements of the variable stators—movable airfoils that controlled the airflow through the compressor. Like all engines at the time, the F100 was controlled by a hydromechanical system, a compact labyrinth of pressure chambers, valves and cams. As the engine saw service, however, the system had to be adjusted for changes in engine performance, a process that called for a full-power ground run, measurements of temperature and many fine adjustments. The F100 required frequent trim runs and even then tended to run hot again after a few flights.

Solving these problems took a great deal of work and some acrimonious disputes between Pratt & Whitney and the Air Force. Some mechanical changes reduced the stagnation problem, but the engine was left with some irksome restrictions on handling and a general lack of durability. In 1979, Pratt & Whitney started development of a new version of the F100, incorporating some major changes.

In the high-pressure turbine, directly downstream from the combustor, the new version had more durable blades produced by a radical new process. Any metal object has a crystalline structure, although it is not usually visible. The boundaries of the crystals are random in a cast-metal object like a turbine blade, and they tend to be the point where components fail. To counter this tendency, metallurgists add a crystal-bonding agent to the exotic nickel-based alloys from which blades are made, but this agent, in turn, lowers the blade's resistance to heat.

It was found in the 1960s, however, that crystal boundaries would only form in straight lines. If a blade, still in its molten state, was withdrawn vertically, root first, from the furnace, it would solidify from the root outward and all the boundaries would be straight. The alloy could then be made up with less crystal-bonding material.

The next step was to add a small block of metal under the blade mold, linked to it by a pigtail coil. The small block would solidify first, and the crystal boundaries would start to form, but none of them would be able to propagate through the coil. The result: the blade would be a single crystal, and the bonding element could be completely removed. Engineers then made another discovery. If the blade was made in two halves, split along itself, as part of the same single-crystal casting, the two halves of the same crystal could be bonded together under heat and pressure, and would fuse together so perfectly that they could no longer be distinguished from a single component.

To understand the importance of this attribute of single-crystal (SC) blades, it must be remembered that the gas temperatures at the high-pressure turbine—the hottest part of the engine—are higher than any alloy can tolerate. To prevent the turbine

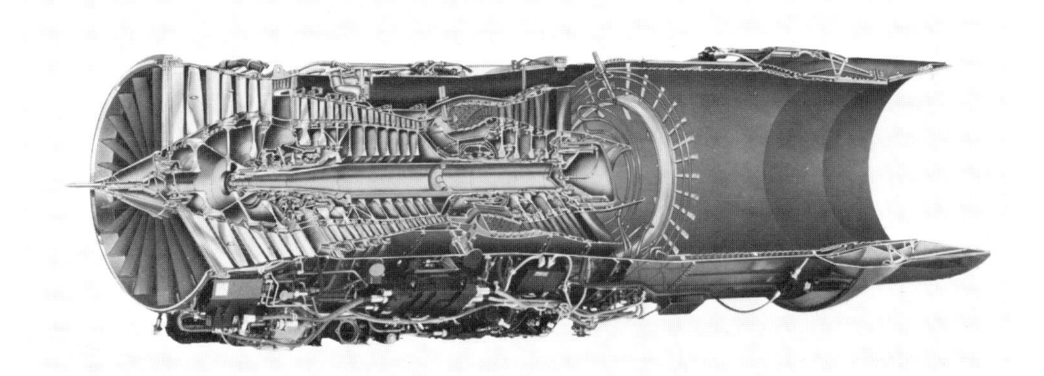

Pratt & Whitney's F100-PW-229 is being developed to provide extra power for the F-15E and F-16C/D. Typical features of the modern fighter engine include the three-stage fan, at the front; the relatively large bypass duct, which surrounds the compressor with its many small blades; and the large augmentor. (Pratt & Whitney)

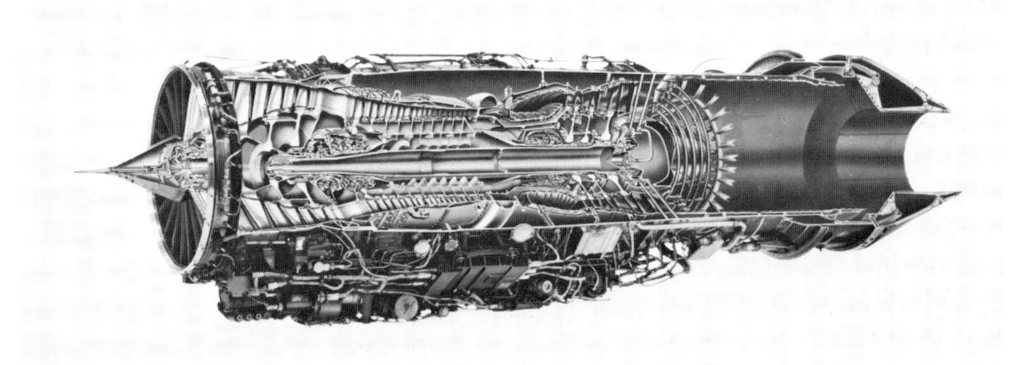

This is the PW1120 engine, which Pratt & Whitney has developed for the IAI Lavi. Note that the bypass duct is much smaller than that of the F100; the ATF engine, with a bypass ratio of 0.2:1, is likely to resemble the PW1120 in that respect. The complex nozzle, with its variable ramps and sliding petals, is designed to vary in area to suit the airflow at different thrust levels while producing minimum drag. (Pratt & Whitney)

from dribbling out of the exhaust, it is warrened with air passages, slots and holes which take cool air from the compressor and use it to form a protective film of air over the blade. Before the SC blade, however, the cooling passages had to be machined out by electron beams, and they had to be relatively simple in design. With the SC blade, however, complex cooling passages could be cast into the inside of the blade, so that it could be more efficiently cooled and endure still hotter temperatures.

Another change to the later F100 version was the use of a digital computer rather than a hydromechanical device to control the engine. This technique is usually known as full-authority digital engine control (FADEC), although Pratt & Whitney calls it digital electronic engine control (DEEC). The advantage of a FADEC system is that its control laws—the rules that determine how it responds to a given control input under given circumstances—can be far more sophisticated than those in a mechanical control system, because they are on a read-only memory chip rather than being built into valves and pressure gauges. FADEC is faster reacting and more precise, can monitor more parameters and can deal with more subtle variations than the mechanical system. It can also be programmed to avoid the combination of circumstances that might lead to a stall. Finally, a FADEC system can monitor the operation of the engine and, in effect, trim it continuously.

SC blades and FADEC are two technical legacies from the F100 program to future fighter engines. There was also a philosophical legacy. Never again would the USAF start the development of a new engine from scratch at the same time as starting development of the airframe and, in the future, all combat engines would be tested more aggressively. Instead of being put through simulated flight cycles, they would be run through successions of throttle slams and retardations, which were much more severe than they would encounter in service. Accelerated mission testing (AMT), as this process is called, is literally intended to break the engine, so that the weak spots are identified before it reaches the squadrons.

Europe had a similarly traumatic experience with an advanced engine in the 1970s. The Anglo-German-Italian Tornado fighter was designed around an entirely new engine, the Turbo-Union RB.199, which proved so troublesome that the flight-test program virtually ground to a halt for two years; the engines were so unreliable that the rest of the aircraft and systems could not be tested in flight.

The F-18's General Electric F404 engine, on the other hand, cruised through development with hardly a hitch. (With one exception; an F-18 was lost in England in September 1978 after a disk failed. The critical missing parts of the disk were never found, the cause remained a mystery, and no similar incident has occurred since.) GE attributed its success to the fact that the F404's ancestor, the GE15/YJ101, had made its first run in 1973 and had been extensively test-flown before the design of the F404 began, while the F404 itself had been one of the first engines to be put through the AMT torture tests.

Because of these experiences, the USAF, the US Navy and the European ministries of defense took care, during the later 1970s, to foster the development of basic technology for the next generation of fighter engines. What emerged, on both sides of the Atlantic, was technology that promised some radical improvements in engine performance and reliability.

The use of computers to model complex airflows has been mentioned before as an important advance in the art of aircraft design. The effects of similar technology on engine design may be even greater. Each of the blades in a turbine engine is an airfoil, but the blade is relatively short and bounded by a solid wall at its root and tip. Up to the 1970s, the complex effects that occur where the flow over the blade interacts with the flow over the inner or outer walls could not be accurately modeled or analyzed. The safe course taken by designers was to increase the aspect ratio of the blades (making them longer in relation to their chord) so that the significance of these end-wall effects could be minimized. However, new technology has made it possible to model the complex three-dimensional flow, and to design workable blades that are shorter in span and longer in chord than those of earlier engines.

The advantages of this approach include the fact that the chunkier blades attach to the disk over a wider area, and because they are shorter they impose lower centrifugal loads on the disk. The disk can therefore be made to spin faster without risking failure, and—like a high-revving car engine—can do more work. Blade loadings can also be increased, because the new blades are thicker and stiffer.

Pratt & Whitney's XF119 made its first run in October 1986. This somewhat uninformative shot is the best that the USAF has been prepared to release for publication. (Pratt & Whitney)

The result is that each stage can generate a much greater rise in pressure than was possible with earlier engines. While it took the F100 ten compressor stages to achieve a 25:1 pressure ratio, a new engine can achieve the same ratio in five stages. The engine can be made much shorter, lighter and stiffer. (The last-mentioned quality is important, because it makes it possible to have very tight clearances throughout the engine and to maintain them in service, improving efficiency.) Because the new-type blades are longer and more twisted than previous blades, not only is the number of stages reduced, but the number of blades on each stage is cut as well. The result is that the total number of blades in the engine is reduced by up to a half.

In the design of the Eurojet EJ200, the jointly developed engine for the Eurofighter EFA, the partner companies—Rolls-Royce, MTU of Germany, Fiat and Spain's SENER—have decided to apply the near-term technology discussed above. Compared with the F404, which is roughly the same size, the EJ200 will be shorter and have a higher thrust/weight ratio, around 10:1. It will also be simpler, with fewer blades, and like the latest version of the F100 it will have SC turbine blades and digital control.

As the USAF approached the design of the ATF engine, however, it was clear that the requirement would be more demanding, because the aircraft was required to cruise and maneuver at supersonic speed. Granted, the maximum speed would be little if any higher than that of the F-15, but that—as the engine designers soon realized—was not the difficult part.

Basically, current fighters are subsonic aircraft with a supersonic dash capability. They can only exceed the speed of sound by using augmented thrust, which consumes so much fuel that it can be used for no more than a few minutes in any one

An early mockup of the Pratt & Whitney XF119, with its two-dimensional vectoring nozzle. Overall, the engine is shorter than the F100, and weighs about the same. (Pratt & Whitney)

mission. As the augmentor is opened up to its maximum boost, not only does thrust increase further, but the SFC, or the amount of fuel for each pound of thrust, increases as well, peaking at up to three times its normal level. The result is that the maximum listed speed of any fighter is very rarely attained in service.

Another effect of supersonic speed is more subtle. The inlet system of a fighter aircraft is carefully designed to decelerate the high-speed airflow entering the intake (actually, of course, the air is static and the airplane is moving, but it is easier to think of the air as moving when discussing inlets) and compress it, so that it can expand on the way out of the engine and generate thrust. At supersonic speeds, this compression effect is powerful enough to heat the incoming air by a significant amount. This temperature rise is then multiplied by the pressure ratio of the engine, so the increase in temperature at the compressor exit is even greater. At a certain speed, which varies with the engine's pressure ratio, the flow of fuel to the combustor has to be cut back, or the combustor-exit temperature will exceed permissible limits and the turbine will be damaged. The result is that the SFC increases, the thrust/weight ratio declines, and the aircraft rapidly reaches a point where it has little power left for acceleration or maneuver.

Very fast aircraft, such as the Soviet MiG-25, and supersonic-cruise aircraft like the SR-71 and Concorde, get around this problem by using engines with a moderate pressure ratio combined with efficient inlet systems. Such powerplants work well at high speed, but are comparatively heavy and inefficient at low speeds. The USAF wanted the ATF to match the supersonic maneuver performance of its conventional fighters, so that approach was out of the question. Instead, the ATF engine would simply have to run hot. The exact maximum operating temperature to be reached by the ATF engine is classified, but is thought to be about as big an advance over the F100 as that engine represented over the previous generation.

Because ATF requirements would push the state of the art in engine design so hard, the USAF and the manufacturers took early action in two main areas to avert any repetition of the F100 problems. One of these was to commission new test facilities to simulate environments never before simulated.

One of the snags in developing an advanced engine has been that, very often, the only device that will turn an advanced compressor at its design speed is the turbine that will drive it in the aircraft. It would be preferable, and would help to avoid some unpleasant surprises, if components could be tested before the complete engine was assembled.

The USAF accordingly renovated a massive 1940s propeller test facility at Wright-Patterson AFB, fitted with a 25,000 horsepower electric motor, to test compressors at full speed. Pratt & Whitney, meanwhile, built a test system in which a J58 engine was used to force air into experimental high-pressure spools, so that they could be tested under operational conditions before they were built into the rest of the engine. To test complete engines and inlet systems, the USAF overhauled its massive facilities at Tullahoma, Tennessee, until they could accurately duplicate the pressures and temperatures encountered at Mach 2.5 and 70,000 feet.

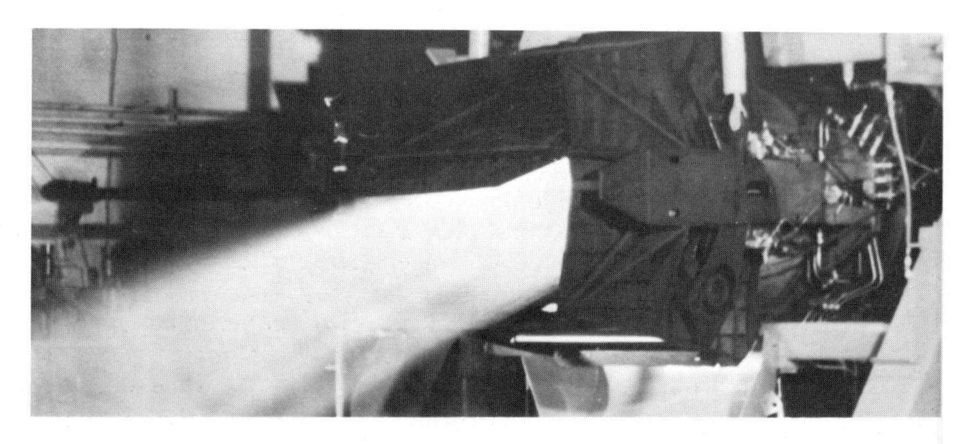

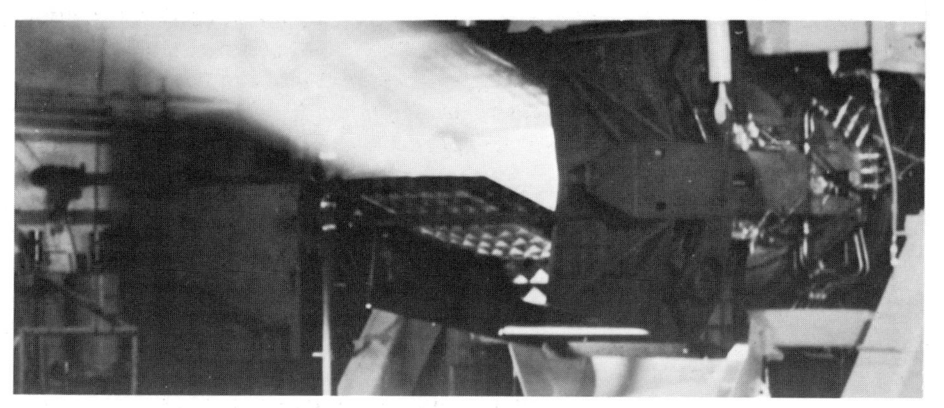

Late in 1982, Pratt & Whitney ground-tested a prototype vectoring and reversing nozzle on an F100. This sequence shows how the full augmented thrust of the engine could be vectored thirty degrees upward or downward. Lighter, "flight-weight" nozzles using the same principle are used on the F-15 SMTD demonstrator. (Pratt & Whitney)

The other important step taken by the USAF was to define most of the performance requirements for the engine as early as possible. The ATF engine specification was firm by the summer of 1983, well before the final details of the fighter itself were pinned down. While this move entailed some risk – time and money might be lost if the fighter specification changed for some reason – it meant that the engineers could start work early on engines with the same size and cycle as the production powerplant. The engine was then called the Joint Advanced Fighter Engine (JAFE), because there was still some Navy interest in the program. However, the Navy had just dropped its plans for the VFMX multirole aircraft, and its need for JAFE was diminishing. (The Navy's new bomber, the ATA, is reportedly powered by improved F404s.)

The USAF issued a request for proposals covering JAFE in May 1983, indicating that two contractors would be selected for the program. General Motors' Allison division did submit a bid, but there was never any serious doubt that God was on the side of the big battalions; the giants of the business, General Electric and Pratt & Whitney, were selected in the following September. In 1986, the program was renamed, and is now known as ATF Engine (ATFE).

Discussion of the ATFE program is complicated by the fact that it has always been more closely classified than the ATF itself. The program office has neither given any unclassified briefings on the program, nor permitted the contractors to do so, since Pratt & Whitney and General Electric went on contract. Most of the information that follows was obtained in briefings in the spring of 1983, before the lid came down on the program; fortunately, there is no sign that requirements have changed substantially since then.

The structure of the program appears to draw on the success of engines like the F404, with demonstrator engines being built and extensively tested, under realistic conditions, in time for results to be fed into the design of preproduction engines. Pratt & Whitney's demonstrator, the PW5000 (Air Force designation is XF119) ran in October 1986, and the GE37, or XF120, is believed to have made its first run shortly afterward. These engines are not designed to be flown, and specification weights are not sacrosanct, but will prove the aerodynamics of the engine and ensure that temperatures and stresses accord with design levels. Also, production-type components can be fitted into the demonstrators and tested before the complete engines are ready.

In 1988, the first preproduction YF119 and YF120 engines are due to run, and will be used for two purposes: accelerated mission testing, to verify that the engine will be durable and reliable in service, and flight-worthiness tests, in preparation for flight trials aboard the ATF prototypes. Both ATFE teams are under some pressure, because the USAF's decision in 1986 to fly competing ATF prototypes in 1990, rather than selecting an ATF winner on the basis of ground tests, means that flight-worthy engines must be available two years earlier than previously expected.

The ATF engines will be slightly more powerful than the F100 or F110, developing about 20,000 pounds of thrust on military power (full thrust without afterburner) and 30,000 pounds of thrust with full reheat. The pressure ratio will be about the same, but will be attained in many fewer stages. Largely because of this, the ATFEs will weigh only 3,000 pounds or so, less than the F100 and considerably less than the F110; thrust/weight ratio, therefore, will be 10:1, compared with 8:1 for the F100 and 7.3:1 for the F110.

These advances seem modest; where the engine breaks new ground is in supersonic performance. The ATFE is required to develop some sixty percent more military (unreheated) power at supersonic speeds than current engines, equivalent to a doubled thrust/weight ratio.

The two engines are thought to be rather different in basic design. Pratt & Whitney's YF119 is believed to be a low-bypass turbofan, with a bypass ratio of 0.2:1; out of every twelve pounds of air entering the inlet, ten pounds goes into the high-pressure compressor and two pounds is fed directly into the augmentor. The choice

The sheer precision and strength of a jet engine's manufacture is impressive. (Pratt & Whitney)

of bypass ratio is a compromise based on desired engine characteristics. The previous generation of fighter engines had higher bypass ratios, which provide a slower, more efficient propulsive jet at subsonic speeds and make it possible to boost thrust by up to seventy percent in the augmentor. For supersonic cruising flight, the best solution is a "pure turbojet" without any bypass. However, the ATF requirement sets tough targets for high supersonic dash speeds and supersonic maneuverability and acceleration, which in turn call for more augmented thrust than a pure jet can provide. Basically, therefore, the YF119 has a minimum bypass ratio set by the need to cool the augmentor and to supply it with oxygen for combustion.

The rival YF120 has been described as more exotic than the YF119. In an interview in 1983, a General Electric official said that the company was looking closely at making the ATF powerplant a variable-cycle engine (VCE), using techniques drawn from research into supersonic transport engines. In a VCE, the bypass ratio can be changed according to the flight conditions. The system that General Electric was studying at the time was a variable-area bypass injector (VABI); a variable-area nozzle located between the turbine and the augmentor, which would increase the exit throat of the bypass duct while reducing the core exit area, or vice versa. The VCE engine, at that time, offered three to four percent more thrust in the critical transonic and supersonic regime, together with greater subsonic thrust and improved subsonic fuel consumption. None of the improvements was massive by itself, but together could make a very significant difference in the performance of the aircraft.

Another new feature being demonstrated under the ATF program is the vectoring and reversing nozzle, being tested as a prototype on the F-15 SMTD. The challenge, in this case, is to integrate such a nozzle into the engine within the specified weight, and this has proven difficult. The nozzle is rectangular in shape, whereas for minimum weight a nozzle has to be round. (It is a pressure vessel, and physics and structural mechanics dictate that round pressure vessels are more efficient.) It also has a complex and inevitably heavy actuation system. The reverser also absorbs the full blast of the exhaust, and heat is a major problem.

In the SMTD reverser, Pratt & Whitney has had to adapt turbine-cooling techniques to cool the reverser panels, but this requires a tremendous flow of cooling air; some of the pipes in the SMTD system are as much as four inches in diameter. The question is whether this type of nozzle can be made sufficiently light and efficient so that it does not detract from performance in normal "up-and-away" flight.

Both the F119 and F120 are likely to feature some similar new techniques. Low-aspect-ratio blades, as noted earlier, make it possible to design a simpler compressor and, in the turbine, allow shorter, fatter blades which are easier to equip with efficient internal cooling systems. However, such blades have one drawback: because they are short in relation to their chord, maintaining tight clearances between the blades and the case becomes even more important than is usually the case on a high-pressure-ratio engine. New engines are likely to feature "active clearance control," in which cooling air is fed to ducts around the case at high engine temperatures, fractionally shrinking the case and counteracting the tendency for clearances to open up as the engine warms up. The F119 compressor may use a version of Pratt & Whitney's Thermatic system, in which warm air is fed to the inside of the compressor rotor, which expands to fit the enlarged case.

The ATF engines will mainly use materials evolved from those in use today: alloys of titanium for the casing, compressor blades and disks, and high-temperature nickel alloys for turbine blades. However, it is possible that a new form of composite material, reinforced carbon-carbon (RCC), may find a use in some parts of the engine. RCC is produced by laying up carbon fibers in a special matrix that carbonizes when heated. The advantage of RCC is that it is not only light and strong, but it is also virtually impervious to heat, being able to survive temperatures well above 3,000 degrees Fahrenheit without cooling. Used to line the augmentor, it would save weight and a good deal of cooling air, allowing the engine to run more efficiently. The disadvantage of RCC is that it is combustible, and, while it is possible to apply protective fire-resistant coatings to RCC, it is worrisome to have such coatings be the only thing in the way of a severe engine fire. The situation is less serious in the augmentor, where there is very little oxygen to sustain combustion, and damaged components will, in any event, be blown out of the exhaust.

Stealth affects the engine designer in several ways. As noted in the previous chapter, Stealth probably demands the use of unconventional inlets; one of the reasons for the USAF's expansion of its Tullahoma altitude chambers is probably to permit full-scale engines to be tested behind strange inlets. The engine designer, meanwhile, must produce a compressor that can tolerate variations in pressure across the inlet face without stalling. Visible smoke must be virtually eliminated from the exhaust, a task well within the reach of modern combustor design. The toughest single problem, though, is the heat that any jet engine pumps out with its exhaust. There is no way to eliminate or absorb this energy, but it is apparently possible to "shape" the exhaust plume, through special nozzle design, so that it mixes more quickly with the outside air, reducing its intensity and the range at which it can be detected.

In summary, new technologies are helping to create engines that seem to have the best of everything: improved maintenance characteristics, high thrust/weight ratio and excellent high-speed performance. However, the challenges of high operating temperatures and low observables should keep the engine designers' hair as gray as ever.

Chapter 5

The electronic fighter

Air combat is "like playing a three-dimensional video game, in constant fear of assassination, with the entire Los Angeles Rams football team sitting in your lap." This is the view of Eugene C. Adam, McDonnell Douglas Aircraft's dean of fighter cockpit design. Twelve years ago, Gene Adam designed the advanced cockpit concept that was implemented for the F/A-18, and subsequently adapted—with some modifications—for the F-16C, F-20 and most other new fighters.

Gene Adam now says the F/A-18 cockpit could and should have been flown a dozen years earlier, because both the technology and the need were present in the early 1960s. He also believes that today's technology and tomorrow's needs call for an approach to cockpit design that seems considerably more radical than the F-18's cathode-ray tubes (CRTs) and push-button controls seemed in the mid-1970s.

Adam's view is shared throughout the industry. In the case of the ATF, the question is not whether the cockpit should be redesigned, but how radical a redesign is necessary and how much can be achieved within the limits of time and money. Moreover, the cockpit is no longer being considered simply as a seat and a collection of instruments and controls, but as the center of the fighter's information system: the sensors that gather data on targets and the tactical situation, the onboard systems that store general information and the computers that must make sense of it all and feed it to the pilot.

The problem facing today's pilots is that the rate at which data can be acquired and the rate at which it changes are outrunning the pilot's ability to make sense of the picture. In 1986, an F-15 made its first flight fitted with a new cockpit device, a Joint Tactical Information Distribution System (JTIDS) display. JTIDS is a multipoint digital datalink into which various sensors—such as ground-based and airborne radars, and electronic surveillance systems—feed data on targets. This data can then be accessed by any user. The USAF originally planned to put a miniature JTIDS terminal on each F-15, but encountered a problem. The JTIDS screen, showing a typical selection of targets and events in a 300-mile-square area in Central Europe on a five-inch CRT, looks like the Lord's Prayer written on the back of a postage stamp, in Icelandic runes. The plan to equip the single-seat F-15 with JTIDS was dropped in late 1986, although the Navy plans to put it in its two-seat F-14D.

Even the latest cockpits do only a mediocre job of relaying information to the pilot. The total CRT area, which is the only means of displaying tactical situation data, is smaller than the usable screen area of a personal computer, so that sensor information must be either miniaturized or eliminated to fit the space available. The complete tactical picture is divided among three CRT displays, which are on different scales and may not be in real-world proportions. (The latter observation applies to the radar display, which is distorted to present the radar's conical field of view on a square screen.)

The ATF will make the problems worse. To begin with, its supersonic cruising speed means that the tactical situation will unfold at least fifty percent faster than it does in an F-15. At the same time, the space available for displays will if anything be reduced, because the pilot will occupy a reclined position, with his knees intruding on the panel space, and the demands of supersonic drag reduction restrict the cross section of the cockpit.

The ATF will also have new sensors and new sources of information. The radar, under development by Westinghouse and Texas Instruments, will still be the primary sensor. Its performance will be a further advance on current fighter radars, which are already so powerful that they can detect targets well over 100 miles away and, in

Engine performance has a dramatic effect on aircraft performance. In the Grumman F-14A Plus and F-14D, the new F110 engine replaces the original TF30. The re-engined aircraft will be far more maneuverable, because the new engines are lighter and more powerful. The incidence of engine stalls will be reduced, allowing the pilot to use available power more effectively. With the more powerful engines, the new F-14s will be able to leave the carrier without using their afterburners, saving fuel and greatly increasing their range. (Grumman)

The primary sensor aboard ATF and other future fighters will be radar. The size and complexity of a fighter radar is indicated by this view of the Hughes APG-63 fitted to the F-15; after the engines, the radar is the largest and most expensive piece of fixed equipment on the aircraft. (Hughes)

Most modern fighter radars have flat antennas rather than the classic dish; this is the APG-66 fitted to the F-16A. Antenna size is important to aircraft design and radar performance. The F-16 has a slim nose and a proportionally small antenna, so that the radar's power supply and signal processing must be improved to attain good performance. (Westinghouse)

some cases, identify them by counting the first-stage compressor blades in their engines. Instead of a mechanically steered antenna, it will have a "phased array" comprising hundreds of miniature antennas, individually varying their pulse frequencies to steer the main focus of the beam. This should be more reliable than current systems because of the elimination of the mechanical element, but it also makes the radar very flexible; it can change wave bands or waveforms, or use all or part of the array, or even act like two or more smaller arrays.

Compared with previous fighters, ATF will have a much greater ability to detect, classify and locate threats and targets according to their electronic emissions, as a result of increased computer power which permits more subtle processing, and the development of new receiving antennas which are more sensitive to direction than those installed on current fighters.

ATF is also intended to have a new infrared search and tracking system (IRST), under development by General Electric and Martin Marietta, which will be able to detect targets at long range (the exact range is classified, but is not far short of 100 miles at high altitude). IRST is very useful because it makes it possible to detect targets without telltale radar emissions, but its basic drawback is that it provides only bearing and elevation and cannot measure range, or the rate of change in range. Unlike a radar, therefore, it cannot tell if a target presents an immediate threat. Such systems have been susceptible to false alarms in the past, but better processing is expected to alleviate this problem.

Another vastly expanded source of information aboard ATF is the onboard database. Information storage and retrieval technology has advanced to a new plateau with the advent of "optronics," or systems that combine optics with electronics. The most familiar optronic device is the compact disc (CD) player, but CD read-only memory (CD-ROM) devices are beginning to make an impact in the computer world. With a combination of high capacity and fast access times, optronic devices make it possible to store a vast quantity of information aboard the aircraft and to make use of it in real time. For example, the characteristics and lethal envelopes of hostile SAMs and AAMs could be stored in an optronic device; so could the enemy's complete order of battle. Optronic devices are ideal for storing maps and target information.

It is frustrating to have such a wealth of tactical information available, and yet be unusable because there is no way to present it to the pilot. The first step—but only the first step—in solving the problem is to improve physical displays in the cockpit.

The state-of-the-art fighter cockpit has two kinds of primary display. Above the instrument panel is the head-up display (HUD), which was first put into service in the 1960s. It is a reflective panel on which a CRT, via an optical system beneath the unit, projects symbols or imagery which is superimposed on the real world. The symbols can identify targets, show the pilot his heading, airspeed and attitude and inform him of the status of the aircraft systems. Like a very smart gunsight, it can also help in weapon aiming.

New HUDs, such as the Kaiser unit developed for the F-15E, differ from earlier types in that they use wider, curved reflectors in front of the pilot. To avoid some of the design problems inherent in using conventional reflective optics for such a task, these reflectors use "diffraction" optics. A fine grid, with a spacing in the same order as the wavelength of visible light, is created by exposing a photosensitive film to the coherent light of a laser. This phenomenon produces what is called a "hologram," a diffraction grid that controls light in three dimensions. The advantages of the holographic HUD are, first, that a wide-angle system can be built within a realistic weight limit and, second, that the hologram reflects light very completely in a narrow wave band, and is almost completely transparent outside it. This means that imagery can be clearly displayed on the screen without blocking out the view of the real world beyond it.

The other main display in current cockpits, apart from the HUD, is the multifunction display (MFD), a monochrome CRT screen with a line of push buttons on each side. The pilot can change what is displayed on the MFD, and as he does so the legend corresponding to each push button changes as well.

As in the case of the HUD, some evolutionary improvements are in hand. The MFD is a fairly simple piece of equipment, and the avenues for improvement are fairly well identified. Larger screens could be used, and the use of color would be a great step forward. Adding color to a visual display would increase the "bandwidth" on which it transmits information. The human eye and brain respond instinctively to color; consequently, if the priority of an item on the screen changes, for example, it could be conveyed by a change in color without using another attention-getting device to ensure that the pilot does not overlook it.

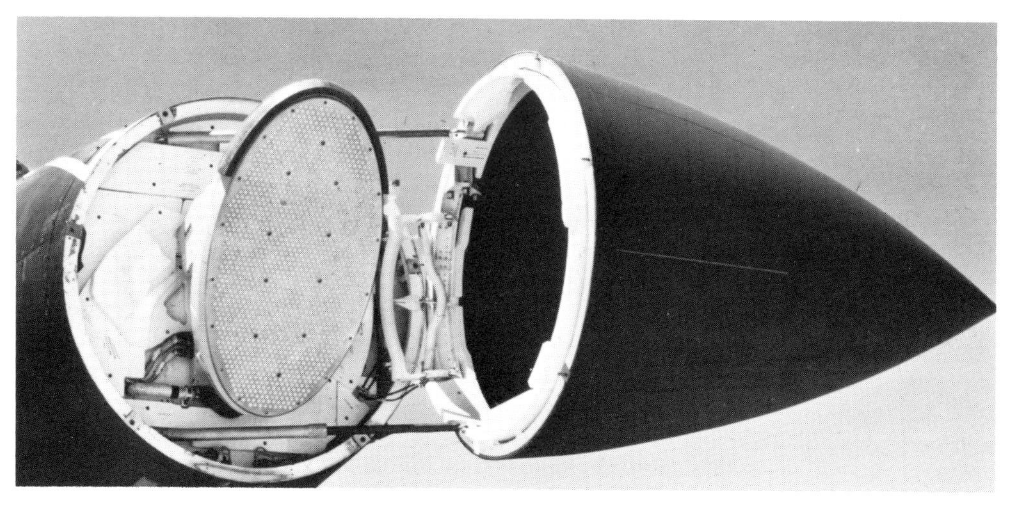

The Westinghouse APQ-164 radar for the B-1B bomber is the first airborne radar to use a phased-array antenna. Westinghouse and Texas Instruments are developing phased-array radar systems for the ATF prototypes; the radars are not quite the same, but will use common components. (Westinghouse)

A phased array consists of hundreds of tiny, synchronized radar transmitters and receivers. To point the beam or change its form, the synchronization between the individual modules is electronically adjusted. Advantages of the phased array include the ability to change the effective shape of the antenna, helping to defeat countermeasures; a high degree of flexibility, allowing the radar to operate in different modes almost simultaneously; and improved reliability, because the high-speed mechanical antenna drive is eliminated and, even if one or more modules should fail, the radar will continue to function. (Westinghouse)

The performance of fighter radars continues to improve. This image of an airfield was obtained at several miles' range, in the late 1970s, by a modified Hughes APG-63. Tests with that radar led to the new APG-70 for the F-15E; this is claimed to offer even better resolution, but results are classified. (Hughes)

The F-14A is equipped with a stabilized, long-focal-length video camera under the nose, to aid in identifying targets outside visual range. ATF will have an electro-optical sensor system (EOSS) produced by General Electric and Martin Marietta, which is likely to combine this type of capability with the functions of an infrared search-and-track sensor. A key advantage of EOSS is that it will be able to detect targets without tell-tale electronic emissions. (Northrop)

Weight and performance in bright sunlight are two current impediments to the use of large-format color displays in fighter aircraft—they are already being used in the larger, shadier cockpits of airliners—but there seems little doubt that the problem will succumb to research work now under way. Flat-panel displays based on plasma or liquid-crystal technology are among the approaches being studied.

A logical step forward from the development of large color displays is the use of pictorial formats for many displays. These are particularly useful for such tasks as weapons management. A typical display might show the plan-view of the aircraft, with its weapons identified by color. Changing colors in the nose of the weapon would indicate, for instance, whether it would be safe, armed, locked-on or selected for release. Such a display would be an enormous advance on present technology, where the pilot has to check the physical position of arming switches before releasing a weapon. The basic advantage of pictorial displays is that they can be comprehended instantly rather than in seconds, time that can be crucial in air combat. In a USAF/Boeing study, one report noted that there are many horror stories of pilots who made accurate attack runs under intense fire, but failed to drop ordnance due to wrongly set switches.

More radical changes to display technology are also likely. The new wide-angle holographic HUDs are useful in air-to-air combat, but their limited field of view covers only a small portion of the area around the aircraft, and does not cover the full

This map, tested aboard the AFTI/F-16, is generated entirely by computer; current map systems use film. Onboard information systems such as this will be increasingly valuable for ATF, because of the enormous amount of information that can be stored and accessed by modern electronic systems. (USAF)

field of view of the radar or the seeker heads on an infrared missile. Now under development to remedy this deficiency are helmet-mounted displays (HMDs) which are directly mounted on the pilot's helmet.

HMDs present a great many technical challenges, but because they are the only way to keep the visual instrument channel open while the pilot has his head moving and "out of the cockpit," as he should at all times if he wants to stay alive, the challenges are being urgently addressed and are at the point of being overcome.

The purpose of the HMD is to supply the pilot with information that may be aircraft-referenced, such as the bounds to the lethal envelope of his own missiles, or space-referenced, such as the direction in which he is looking or the location of a target detected on radar. This means the computer that generates the HMD sym-

The F-18 set the standard for modern fighter cockpits, with its use of multifunction displays (MFDs) and an up-front control (UFC) panel. Using the head-up display, the UFC and an array of small switches on the stick and throttle, the pilot need not remove his hands from the primary flight controls during combat. The bright display in the lower center of the panel is the F-18's moving map. (McDonnell Douglas)

bology has to know where the pilot's head is pointing. In the Kaiser/McDonnell Douglas Agile Eye system, which started tests in 1987, this task is accomplished by a small coil embedded in the helmet and an electromagnetic pickup above it, mounted on an arm extending from the top of the ejection seat. There are problems, including the fact that the cockpit is a noisy electromagnetic environment, but acceptable accuracy has been achieved in ground tests and the system was due to be flown in 1987. This feature makes the HMD useful as a control device as well as a display system; the pilot can move a cursor on a screen, or direct a sensor or missile seeker toward a target, by moving his head.

This is the cockpit of Northrop's private-venture F-20 Tigershark fighter, showing how F-18 design has been reflected in other aircraft. The right-hand MFD is acting as a radar display, and the left-hand display is showing navigation information. The cockpit is relatively uncluttered, but, then again, the F-20 is not a particularly complex aircraft. (Northrop)

Another challenge in HMD design is the optical system, which must be light and unobtrusive, but effective. Some early prototype systems seemed effective until the pilot's helmet shifted slightly on his head, whereupon the HMD image was lost completely and could no longer be recovered, because the pilot had no cues to tell him where to move his head in order to see the image again. In the Agile Eye HMD, weight and bulk are reduced by making the final screen a hologram, built as an integral part of the visor. Another important factor in making HMDs practical has been the development of tiny CRTs, no bigger than a man's finger; the Agile Eye display is produced by one of these, mounted at the rear of the helmet. The image is carried from the CRT across the pilot's head to the visor by an intricate, computer-designed chain of mirrors.

The fact that most service helmet specifications have not been revised to reflect advances in materials and other technology has made it easier to develop HMDs. The

The cockpit of the British Aerospace EAP represents a step beyond the F-18. There are three MFDs instead of two, and the screens are larger; the HUD is a holographic, wide-angle type. The pushbuttons, which appear to be blank, have a matrix of LEDs (light-emitting diodes) in their faces, and change legend and function according to the system mode. Space is also saved by making the backup mechanical instruments smaller and less conveniently located; MFDs have proven reliable in service and the backups are seldom needed. (BAe)

developers of the Agile Eye knew there would be some penalty in weight as a result of adding the visual system to the helmet, but changes in other parts of the helmet—lightweight headphones, a redesigned oxygen mask and a Kevlar shell—mean that the Agile Eye is actually lighter than USAF or Navy standard helmets.

Voice communication is another new avenue in cockpit design. A primitive form of this system was installed in the B-58 Hustler bomber, and carried taped warnings of system problems. Synthetic speech is used in a number of production applications (such as the commercial ground proximity warning system) and presents no basic problems. Now under active investigation is the reverse of speech synthesis: voice recognition, in which the system responds to commands spoken by the pilot.

Progress is being made in this area, but there are two main challenges. One is to expand the system's vocabulary, grammar and syntax base so that it can respond to normal spoken language, rather than forcing the pilot to talk like a robot in order to be understood. The other is to make the system recognize words reliably and accurately under conditions of stress and under high g loadings, when the pilot's voice changes. This is difficult, but it is unfortunately the case that such circumstances are precisely when voice recognition is needed. Late in 1986, tests of a Texas Instruments

Lockheed's electronic copilot (ECOP) is a simulator and demonstrator for advanced cockpit technologies using expert systems, voice interaction and large-format color displays. This view shows a navigation mode, with a computer-generated view of the terrain ahead of the aircraft on the right-hand display. (Lockheed)

This shows the ECOP in "windowing" mode, with conventional instruments, map and radar data all displayed. In the top right-hand corner of the right screen is a tactical situation display like that produced by JTIDS (Joint Tactical Information Distribution System). Note, in the extreme lower right, a pictorial fuel contents display showing that the fuselage tanks are full and that the wing tanks are partly empty. Such a display is far easier to comprehend than a bank of numbers. (Lockheed)

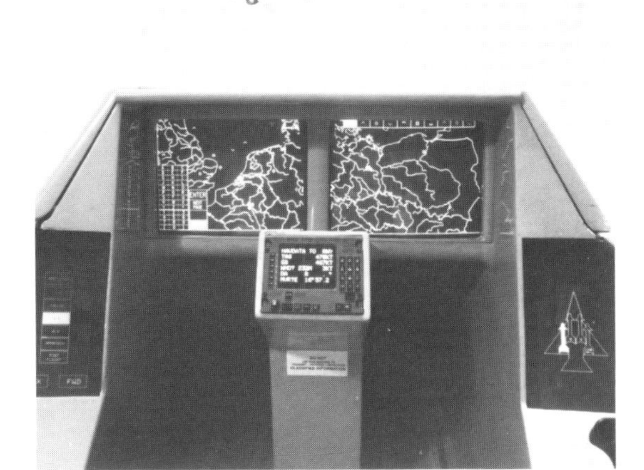

The ECOP is seen in panoramic mode, with the two main screens being used to present a single display. A stores-management display is seen at right, showing that one out of four remaining missiles is ready for firing. (Lockheed)

speech-recognition system on the AFTI/F-16 prototype indicated that the problems were close to solution. Potentially, a combination of a cursor slaved to the HMD and voice control could give the pilot hands-free control over almost any system on the airplane.

Even so, it must be repeated that better display and control hardware are only part of the solution, because today's displays are only part of the problem. Better displays, like improving sensors, will only serve to saturate the pilot faster if other measures are not taken.

Measures of this kind are being studied by the USAF and two contractor teams—one led by Lockheed, and the other headed by McDonnell Douglas, so that each team is linked to one of the ATF projects—under a program called Pilot's Associate (PA). The object of PA is, quite simply, "to provide the pilot with the right information, so that he can intuitively make good decisions," according to a USAF officer in the program, who goes on to stress that optimum, or perfect decisions are not the goal. "The pilot just has to do something reasonable, to keep him out of the position where something automatic has to come in and save him."

But achieving this objective is a lot more difficult than stating it. At first glance, increased automation might seem to be the answer. The trouble with automation, however, is that while it assumes some of the work load, it degrades the pilot's skills,

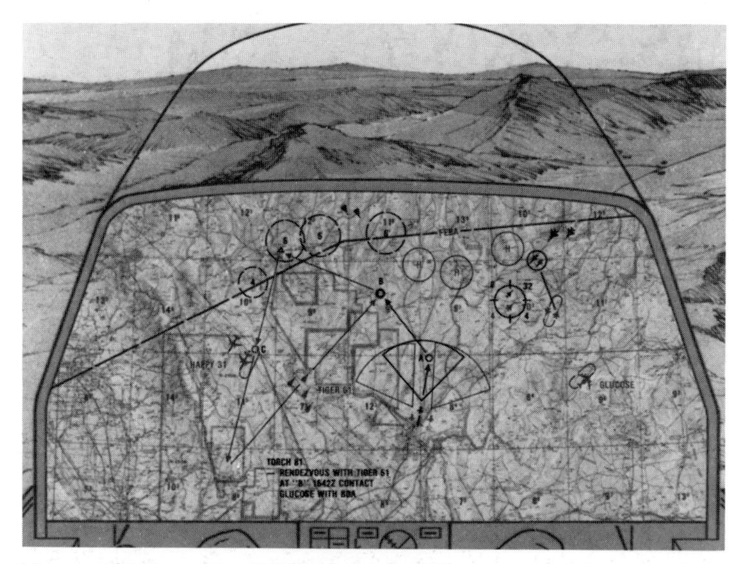

More ambitious than ECOP, and possibly destined for applications farther in the future than ATF, McDonnell Douglas' Big Picture concept is aimed at fusing all onboard, offboard and sensor information into one display that occupies the entire panel. Here, a map display shows the pilot the positions of all other aircraft in the area, the locations and ranges of missile sites (the circles by the battle line) and the intended mission. (McDonnell Douglas)

so that the pilot's abilities and alertness are reduced at the point where they are most needed. When an automatic system takes over, the pilot may not understand why, or realize what is happening, or have any idea what recommendation is coming next, and there will usually be no time for explanations. Also, an automated system must have fixed threshold levels below which it will take no action, so that it does not become saturated itself. The problem here is that the automated system may completely miss an important early event, such as the first sighting of a target or a threat, which an experienced pilot would detect.

PA, instead, relies on new and more flexible techniques made possible by a branch of computer technology known as artificial intelligence (AI) or, perhaps more accurately, "expert systems." Most computer systems are designed to respond to a given input A with result Z. However, this type of system cannot cope with something as wide-ranging as air combat; there are so many variables that it is inconceivable that all of them could be written into one set of software. An expert system is different in that it evaluates inputs according to a set of rules and priorities, and produces a response that is known to work in a similar but not necessarily identical situation. The rules are written by human experts in the task the system is sup-

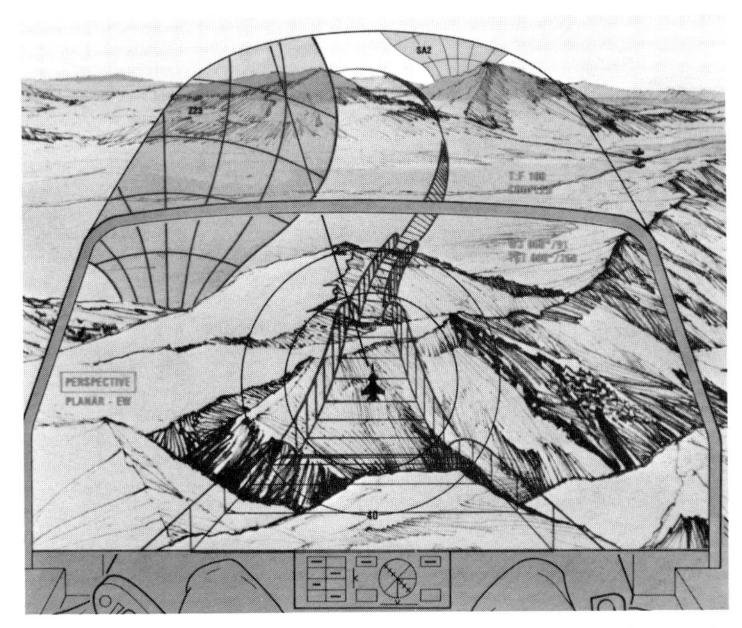

In this "head-forward" display, Big Picture is showing the terrain ahead of a low-flying aircraft. The mushroom shapes are the lethal envelopes of defensive weapons, taking account of terrain masking which limits their range at low altitude. The "highway" track has been selected by the tactical expert system to minimize the attacker's exposure to weapons. (McDonnell Douglas)

posed to perform, with the help of computer simulations and a learning program.

A simple example of an expert system is one that is used to help line maintenance crews locate a fault in a complex electronic system. While it is likely that the line crews have not previously seen this particular set of symptoms, the problem has previously been encountered in development or flight-test and has been written into an expert system by an experienced engineer. The line crew runs the raw outputs from the sick avionics unit through the expert system, which quickly picks out the comparable problem from its knowledge base and proposes a solution.

The key concepts in Pilot's Associate are "adaptive aiding" and "information fusion." The latter is more straightforward, in principle at least. Information fusion involves taking all the inputs from the various sensors on board the aircraft, together with JTIDS and the onboard database, and displaying them in a single format, rather like a fighter pilot's version of the "big board" display in an operations room on the ground. Where the task becomes difficult is where information is incomplete and

Big Picture incorporates touch-screen and voice recognition technology. Here, a pilot is pointing to a SAM site and asking for an assessment of his vulnerability; the system has already identified the lighter-colored area on the map as visible to the SAM. The system responds by marking the track yellow as it crosses the danger area, indicating that there is a 50 percent chance that the SAM crew will detect the aircraft and launch a missile. (McDonnell Douglas)

ambiguous. The ground-based display uses human operators to resolve such problems, but the PA display will use expert systems.

Adaptive aiding is a way of helping the pilot when he needs it, and staying out of the way when no help is needed; the system monitors the pilot's work load, and gradually increases the amount of assistance to the pilot according to the situation. For example, a system that continually prompted the pilot in cruising flight, drawing his attention by visual or verbal means to targets and threats he had noticed but decided to ignore for the time being, would be nothing less than a nagging nuisance. In a more intense situation—if, for example, the pilot was beginning an engagement—he is more likely to miss a newly developing situation such as a technical problem, and the system may be right to prompt him more strongly.

In fact, synthetic voice generation is a companion technology to active aiding. Generating a voice is not at all difficult, but voice has a unique potential for annoyance, unless it is linked to a system that knows when to speak and how much to say,

Windows could be used on Big Picture or similar displays to provide information in different formats. Here, a pilot is preparing to attack a ground target. The main screen shows a map, his aircraft and the area being scanned by the fighter's radar. The radar picture appears in the upper window, and a stores display appears in the lower left-hand corner of the screen. (McDonnell Douglas)

a consideration that applies to humans as well as to computers. ("Are we producing the perfect executive assistant," inquired one engineer about PA, "or the perfect electronic mother-in-law?")

Properly used, voice has a remarkable potential as a broadband communication device, from the near-subliminal reminder that the aircraft is passing a preprogrammed waypoint to the loud, urgent warning of trouble at close quarters. A participant on one of the PA teams was, at one point, seriously considering the use of expletives to add emphasis to particularly urgent warnings; one can only wonder how the Christian right wing of Congress will react when the USAF announces it is spending tax dollars to teach a computer to yell "Break right, you dumb @###**!" in moments of stress.

The system must also move automatically from visual prompts and voice generation to adaptively controlled automation, which differs from conventional automation in that it functions only when it is needed, and starts with the lowest functions first. It can be taken for granted, for example, that the ATF will have a performance management system that constantly corrects the trim, throttle settings and, possibly, the profile of the adaptive wing for minimum fuel consumption at a desired speed. As the situation becomes more intense, the PA system may inform the pilot that it is assuming control of the electronic countermeasures (ECM) system. If the aircraft is pulling high-g combat-type maneuvers, and a target identified as hostile is approaching within lethal range of the ATF's weapons, the PA system may select the appropriate missile and prepare it for launch.

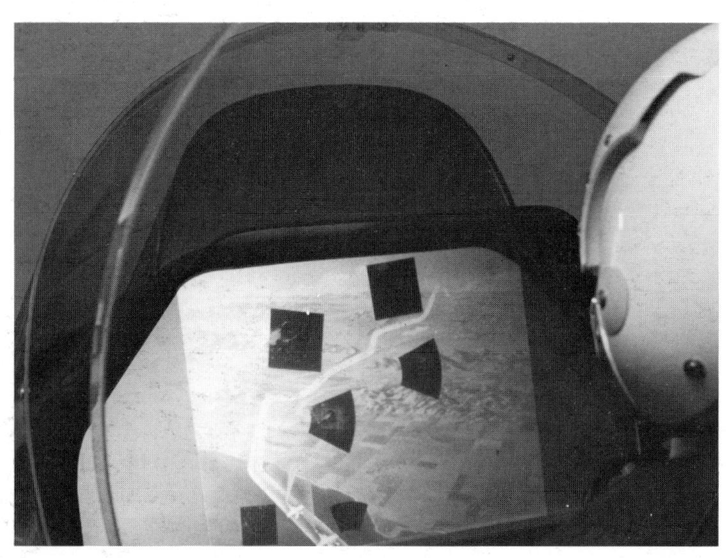

Another use of advanced displays is in mission planning, allowing the pilot to rehearse a mission and preview what he is likely to see. (McDonnell Douglas)

The complexity of the task faced by the PA system means that it will be divided among several expert subsystems, each programmed with the help of a different group of human experts. A "situation assessment" system, for example, would evaluate the tracks, signatures and emissions from targets in the aircraft's vicinity, and cue the pilot's attention to the most imminent threats. "One difference between an ace and an average pilot," notes a member of the PA project office, "is that the ace tends to know what's important for him to gather from all the events going on around him. The inexperienced pilot is out there looking at everything."

Another element of PA would be an expert system concentrating on tactics. While this might suggest a plan of action to a pilot if he requested it, its main function might be to interpret the pilot's control inputs and the movements of the aircraft

An impression of a helmet-mounted display (HMD) shows how basic information can be presented in the pilot's line of sight, in the circular area just to the left of center. Heading, airspeed and basic weapon data are visible, together with a dotted arrow which directs the pilot's attention to a target he can see if he turns his head. (Kaiser Electronics)

for the system. "It's a real problem if the PA system has to ask 'what are you doing?' every ten seconds," says the PA program official.

A pilot/vehicle interface (PVI) expert, also part of the PA system, would manage information fusion, monitor pilot work load and run the displays. Technology developed for sophisticated flight simulators over the past ten years or so will be very important in this area. The "outside world" on a flight simulator used to be made in the form of a scale model of a landmass, measuring perhaps eighty by forty feet, over which a TV camera was moved mechanically. Now, however, more versatile computer-generated image (CGI) systems are used, in which the landmass exists only as millions of picture elements (pixels) on a computer storage device, and is reconstructed continuously as the viewpoint moves. (CGI is being used on an increasing scale to produce special effects in the movie industry.) In the PA cockpit, simulation and reality will merge, as CGI techniques are used to construct vividly colored, fused real-time displays on the MFDs, HUD and HMD.

The pilot's ability to view the world on a clear fused display should vastly improve his ability to manage the long-range air battle, while the HMD should improve his 360 degree awareness in close combat. However, one does not need to be too cynical to wonder how all this technology will work in service, and how it will ever be implemented within the weight and cost limits of a practical fighter airplane. The tough

Simulators such as this are used to test new cockpits and information systems in realistic tactical environments. The mockup cockpit is placed in the center of a 28-foot dome. Projection units, on the gantry above the cockpit, project a computer-generated picture of the outside world on the dome. In many facilities, two domes can be linked together to simulate two-aircraft missions. (General Electric)

maintenance and logistics requirements set for the ATF avionics system—for instance, the elimination of an intermediate shop for support—make the problem even tougher.

Working in favor of the USAF, however, is the explosive increase in computing power, per dollar and per pound, that has taken place since the last generation of air-

The explosion in computer power has made it possible to create scenes of near-photographic quality in simulators, and to change them in real time; as the pilot steers the aircraft, the view changes, just as it would in real life. This picture was generated by a General Electric Compu-Scene IV, a top-of-the-line image generator designed for research and development work. (McDonnell Douglas)

A Lockheed engineer checks images of aircraft which will be used in the company's development simulators. Designing such images is a matter of art as well as science, and a great deal of ingenuity goes into obtaining the maximum realism with the minimum load on the computer. (Lockheed)

craft was designed, and which continues. A related technology is the "databus," a single cable which connects all the different electronic boxes in the aircraft and replaces hundreds of individual sets of wires. Electronic codes direct packages of electronic information (the "passengers" on the bus) to the appropriate "stop." A program originally known as Pave Pillar, and more recently as ASA (Advanced Systems Architecture) is aimed at exploiting this technology to meet the requirements of advanced combat aircraft.

Briefly, ASA exploits the power of modern electronics to implement different functions in similar hardware. Each of the expert systems in the PA group—the control of communications, navigation and identification, electronic warfare functions and so on, all of which are software packages—would be hosted by identical computer modules, each incorporating a processor, a diagnostic unit and a high-speed databus interface. This should reduce acquisition cost, because the standardized modules can be produced in larger numbers, and will also cut the number of spares required. ASA is also intended to provide a high degree of redundancy and an unprecedented self-diagnosis capability, through the diagnostic system built into each module. Redundancy and diagnostics should complement each other, so that the avionics system can detect a fault and re-allocate critical functions among healthy hardware modules. On the ground, the diagnostic system will be linked to a handheld terminal carried by each maintenance worker.

Using so much identical hardware should reduce the cost of building each ATF avionics system, but it will not reduce the cost of developing it. Instead, the burden will be shifted from hardware to software; the ATF system is expected to require twice as many lines of software as the $250 million, 200 ton B-1B bomber. Writing software for a military aircraft is a special problem, because there are no second chances. An undetected software error that would simply mean a few hours of debugging work on a ground-based program could abort a vital mission, lead to the loss of an aircraft or, at worst, kill a pilot if it occurred aboard an aircraft. Producing and validating software is time consuming, and it has been at the root of serious delays in many military aircraft and electronics projects.

In the case of the ATF, the best safeguard against such problems is time. For the first time, the USAF has required the manufacturers to build complete prototype avionics systems alongside their prototype aircraft (which will not, however, fly with complete systems aboard); the Lockheed/Boeing/General Dynamics team intends to fly its complete system aboard a Boeing 757 jetliner. As the production ATF is developed, the avionics prototypes, in conjunction with highly capable simulators, will be used to refine software for the Pilot's Associate and other vital systems.

Early in 1987, the commander of USAF Systems Command, General Lawrence A. Skantze, disclosed that the USAF would spend $900 million on avionics during the ATF prototype stage, more than on either the engine or the airframe, and that one contractor was estimating that avionics would account for forty percent of the fighter's fly-away cost ($14 million in 1985 money). "It's clear that we know how to build an aircraft that can maneuver and fight, and has a low radar cross section. The real difference, and the real leverage in combat, comes from the avionics."

Chapter 6

Weapons

Some time in late 1989, a wing of USAF F-15C fighters will become two to four times more effective without any major aircraft modifications. The only way to tell the more effective fighter from another F-15C will be to look carefully at the missiles on its fuselage weapon stations. Slightly more slender than the usual AIM-7 Sparrow missiles, they will be USAF/Hughes AIM-120 AMRAAMs (advanced medium-range air-to-air missiles).

AMRAAM will be the main armament of the F-15's successor, the ATF, into the foreseeable future. Because it has been adopted as a standard NATO weapon, it will also be carried by the F-16, the F-18, Royal Air Force Tornado interceptors, Royal Navy Sea Harriers and, from 1995, the Eurofighter EFA. It is undoubtedly one of the most important of all Western weapon programs, if not the most important.

To understand why AMRAAM is so badly needed it is necessary to look at its predecessor. The AIM-7 was originally developed by the US Navy to shoot down enemy bombers and attack aircraft before they could launch their own guided weapons at Navy ships; the theory was that the bombers would be nearly as fast as the Navy's fighters, so that closing in and maneuvering to attack them with guns would waste too much time.

Work on the Sparrow started in the late 1940s, and the first version to be produced on a large scale, the Sparrow III, went into service in 1957. The advanced radar and fire-control system of the McDonnell F-4 Phantom was designed to work with the Sparrow, and the aircraft carried four missiles in tailored troughs underneath the fuselage. As a result, the Sparrow was adopted along with the F-4 by the USAF, the Royal Air Force, Germany, Japan, Israel and the many other F-4 customers, and became NATO's standard medium-range AAM.

Because of the emphasis on short-range air-to-air combat in the definition of the F-15, the USAF decided to continue using the AIM-7 as the new fighter's standard medium-range weapon, rather than designing a brand-new missile, eventually developing the new AIM-7M version to overcome problems with earlier subtypes. British Aerospace, in a parallel but separate program, combined new British components with the Sparrow airframe to produce the Sky Flash for RAF Phantoms and Tornado F.2/F.3 interceptors.

While the AIM-7M and Sky Flash are completely different in detail from the original Sparrow III, they are similar in size and configuration and use the same guidance

An AIM-7F Sparrow missile leaves a Northrop F-20 Tigershark. The size and bulk of the missile contrast with the small size of the F-20, and require specially designed pylons. AIM-9L Sidewinders are carried on wingtip rails. (Northrop)

An F-15 launches a Sparrow over the Gulf of Mexico. The solid rocket motor of an AAM burns for a few seconds, after which the missile glides to its target. At extreme range, the missile may have little energy left when it reaches its target, and may be eluded by a sudden maneuver. (USAF)

principle. Both of them weigh about 500 pounds and have fixed tail fins and movable wings for control, like the Sparrow III. This tends to limit the missile's agility, so that, at its maximum range, it may be unable to follow a target that pulls a last-minute evasive maneuver.

The AIM-7M and Sky Flash are, like Sparrow, semi-active radar homing (SARH) weapons. The missile's nose contains a radar receiver or seeker, which detects and homes in on radar energy transmitted by the launch aircraft and reflected by the target. Given the relative bearing and elevation of the target and the rate at which these change—parameters determined by the guidance system from the seeker inputs—the missile navigates a course toward collision with the target.

SARH technology has been steadily refined over the years, to the point where such missiles are accurate, reasonably reliable and highly resistant to jamming. Both weapons have a maximum launch range of about sixty miles, under ideal conditions. These conditions include a head-on engagement, so that the missile need not maneuver very hard and the distance between the launch point and the impact point is reduced by the target's closing speed; a launch at high speed, at an altitude which is equal to or greater than the target's; a reasonably large radar target which does not perform an effective evasive maneuver; and an absence of effective jamming. The launch range decreases as these parameters diverge from their optimum values. The missile's range is much lower if it has to chase a target from astern, for instance, and a beam attack against a maneuvering target may be even more difficult.

The fundamental problem with semi-active missiles, however, is that the launch aircraft's radar must illuminate the target continuously from launch until missile impact, exactly like a microwave-frequency searchlight beam. As long as its radar is locked onto the target and illuminating, it cannot see any other targets. The pilot is therefore in the unpleasant position of running blindly toward the enemy until the missile hits the target, and is vulnerable to attack by other aircraft in the hostile formation.

A critical figure in this kind of engagement is the "F-pole," which is the distance between the launch aircraft and the target when the missile hits and the attacker is free to maneuver and search for other targets. In a head-on engagement between two high-speed targets, the F-pole may be no more than a fraction of the missile's publicly quoted "maximum range," and may well be within the maximum range of a passive, heat-seeking missile. The result, simulations and combat experience have shown, is that a semi-active missile engagement almost invariably leads into a short-range dogfight in which, if anything, the SARH shooter is at a disadvantage.

AMRAAM has a completely different guidance system. In place of a passive radar seeker, its seven-inch-diameter fuselage contains a highly miniaturized radar, essentially similar to a small fighter radar with automatic search and lock-on functions. It has a pulse-Doppler mode, so that it can pick out targets against ground clutter with some reduction in range, and it can also home on radar-jamming energy radiated by the target. The missile's forward fuselage also contains a small inertial reference system, and a datalink receiver is installed in the tail. These three elements are coordinated by an onboard computer.

Immediately before launch, the missile's computer is "initialized" with the position of the target. Its computer and inertial reference system begin to steer it toward that position. The launch aircraft, meanwhile, continues to track the target, and periodically transmits its latest position to the missile. From this information, the missile's onboard computer extrapolates the target's track, predicts its position at impact and determines the fastest and most efficient course to follow to reach that point. As each new target position arrives from the launch aircraft, the missile further refines its course. Up to fifteen miles from the target (the actual range is dependent on the target's RCS), the missile's own radar locks on and completes the interception.

The most important advantage of this guidance technique is that the launch aircraft does not have to illuminate the target with a continuous beam, but needs only to track it. Early fighter radars had to "lock on" to a target in order to track it; the antenna physically followed the target through changes in bearing and elevation, so the radar could not search for other targets or track more than one at a time. Since the F-14 and F-15, however, the standard for performance has been "track-while-scan," in which the radar follows a search pattern and a built-in computer compares the positions of targets in successive scans and constructs their tracks.

Not only does this mean that the radar can continue to search—albeit within a smaller volume of sky—while an AMRAAM is in flight, but, if the radar has enough processing capacity, several targets can be tracked simultaneously. The datalink from

The optical head of an AIM-9 Sidewinder collects infrared (IR) radiation for a sensitive electrical detector. Future IR missiles will have internal arrays of micro-miniaturized detectors, and will be more discriminating and harder to deceive.

the fighter to the missile can be coded and time-shared among several missiles, so the AMRAAM fighter can engage more than one target at a time. The number of targets that can be engaged concurrently is not limited by the missile, but by the radar and datalink hardware and tactical considerations. An F-15C, for example, would probably be electronically capable of a four-on-four AMRAAM launch, but the right conditions for such an engagement would probably be rare.

The other basic advantage of AMRAAM over a semi-active weapon is that the missile can "go autonomous" partway through its flight, requiring no further guidance from the launch aircraft. Conservatively speaking, this point may be reached when the missile's radar locks onto the target; however, the last truly necessary update is earlier in the flight, at the point where the missile's own inertial navigation system is fully capable of taking it within seeker range of the target. Determining this point accurately and reliably involves calculating a large number of variables, including the target's RCS and maneuver history and the missile's remaining energy. However, the result is that the launch aircraft is free to maneuver in any direction, and to resume a maximum-range radar search, long before reaching the classic "F-pole."

The AMRAAM's homing system is extremely accurate, and because of the missile's tail control surfaces it can maneuver very rapidly close to the target, deriving lift from its ogival nose and its body as well as from its wings. As a result, the missile can be expected to pass closer to the target, and the size of the proximity-fuzed blast/fragmentation warhead, compared to that of the Sparrow, can be considerably reduced. Its actual mass has not been published, but is probably around half that of the eighty-eight-pound warhead on the AIM-7. This, together with miniaturization of the electronics, is why it has been possible to make AMRAAM slimmer and thirty percent lighter than the AIM-7, while maintaining approximately the same maximum range

The only active-radar-homing missile in the current NATO inventory is the Hughes AIM-54 Phoenix, carried exclusively by the US Navy's F-14. Its cost, size and weight preclude its use by smaller aircraft. (Grumman)

and significantly increasing its speed. The importance of higher speed is that the missile reaches its point of autonomy more quickly, increasing the distance between the launch aircraft and the target at the point where, from the attacker's point of view, the engagement is complete.

AMRAAM has an alternative "launch-and-leave" mode, which can be used if the target is within range of the missile's radar. Range in this mode is about fifteen miles, considerably less than the weapon's maximum range, but radar guidance may give it a greater launch range and higher kill probability than a conventional short-range missile under some circumstances; in haze or cloud, for instance, or if the target is against the sun. If the pilot is drawn into a short-range fight, this alternative AMRAAM mode means that his medium-range weapons are still useful. Semi-active weapons are little more than dead weight when the fur starts to fly at close quarters.

In computer-simulated combats against aircraft equipped with Sparrow (representative of semi-active weapons in general), aircraft armed with AMRAAM launched their weapons, guided them to the point where they became autonomous, and broke off before entering the lethal envelope of the AIM-7s launched by their opponents "under almost any scenario" according to the USAF.

Not only does the new AIM-120 AMRAAM use active-radar homing, but it is also considerably lighter than the AIM-7. The F-16 can carry up to six AIM-120s, but would more usually carry four, as shown here, together with AIM-9s on the wingtip stations. (General Dynamics)

A USAF F-16 launches an AMRAAM during early trials. Note that the missile's new motor produces much less smoke than the AIM-7 motor thanks to advances in solid-propellant technology. This is important, because the smoke from a rocket can cue the enemy to expect a missile and prepare for an evasive maneuver. (USAF)

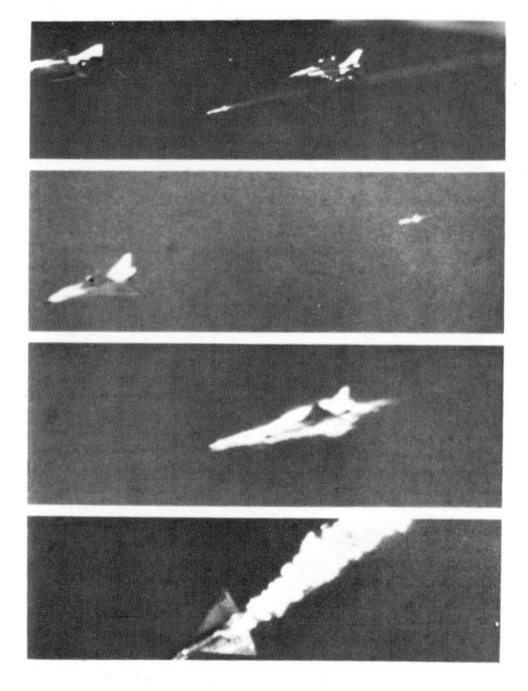

An AMRAAM prototype destroys a QF-102 drone after launch from an F-16. This may not have been the intended result of the test. Physically hitting the target with an AAM is difficult, so most missiles have blast/fragmentation warheads and smart proximity fuzes to disable the target (by rupturing fuel tanks, for instance) without a direct hit. Test missiles usually carry no warhead, but are instrumented to measure the miss distance. In this case, however, the missile scored a direct hit and killed the target by kinetic energy and fire. (USAF)

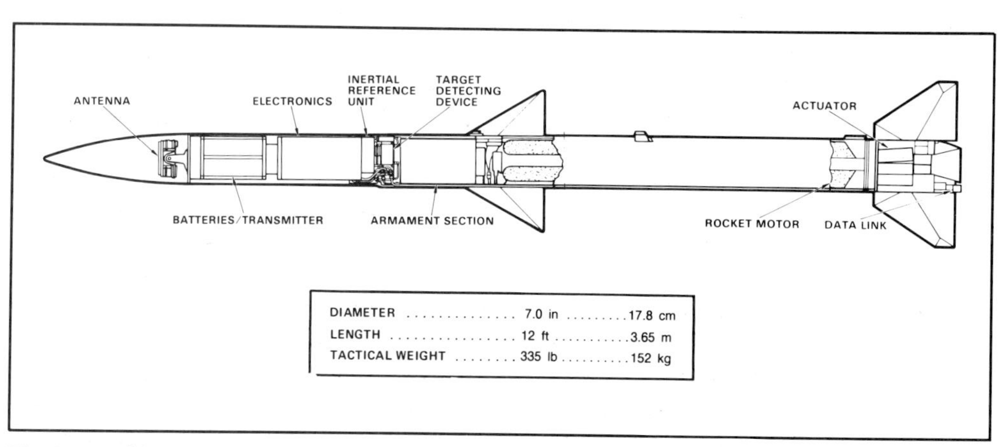

The internal layout of the AIM-120 AMRAAM shows that most of the missile's length consists of motor and electronics. Packaging the radar transmitter and power source in a seven-inch tube proved to be a very difficult development task. The target detection device is an advanced form of proximity fuze which detonates the warhead as the missile passes closest to the target. (Hughes)

Its best friends would not claim that AMRAAM development has been smooth; indeed, the entire program was in disastrous shape at one time, due to overoptimism and some poor technical judgments. After several years of study and two years of technology demonstration, the full-scale development contract was awarded in December 1981. Major problems soon surfaced. The task of developing the radar—compared, at one point, to that of cramming an F-16A radar into a seven-inch tube—proved particularly difficult, and it became clear by the end of 1984 that AMRAAM was going to miss its scheduled service-entry date by a mile. Under pressure from Congress and the Pentagon, the Air Force revised its plans to allow more time for development, and wrote revised contracts under which a series of critical flight tests had to be completed successfully before production funds could be released. Most of those tests had been completed at the time of writing, including tests of the missile's ability to track through chaff (particularly low-altitude chaff against sea clutter), and a look-down, shoot-down shot against ECM. It had distinguished between clustered targets, accurately followed targets through mid-course and terminal maneuvers, and completed a successful track-while-scan launch from an F-16.

The next stage in AMRAAM development is likely to involve producibility improvements; the design of some components goes back to the late 1970s, and some circuits can now be replaced by large-scale integrated (LSI) components. However, such changes are being deliberately delayed until the baseline configuration is proven. Also under study is a "compressed carriage" version of the missile, with folding wings and fins, designed to fit in the ATF's internal missile bay.

The complement to AMRAAM, which is also to be adopted NATO-wide under the same multinational agreement, is the AIM-132 ASRAAM (advanced short-range air-to-air missile), which is under development by British Aerospace and Bodensee Geraten-Technik (BGT) of Germany. ASRAAM has to meet a tough standard: it is intended to replace the AIM-9 Sidewinder, which has endured several efforts to replace it during its thirty-five-year career.

Originally cobbled together from five-inch unguided rocket components by a group of US Navy rocket engineers, Sidewinder has survived for two reasons: it has been continuously developed with improved homing systems, new warheads and other refinements, and it has consistently worked more reliably than any other missile. Its most successful action was in the 1982 Falklands war, when Royal Navy Sea Harriers destroyed nineteen Argentine aircraft in twenty-three missile engagements, an eighty-two percent success rate. The AIM-9L variant, used in the Falklands, represents the state of the art in infrared (IR) air-to-air missiles. Whereas earlier versions of the AIM-9 were designed to home onto the intense IR radiation emitted by the red-hot metal of an adversary's jetpipe, the AIM-9L has a seeker in which the heat-sensitive element is cooled to subzero temperatures by a miniature cryogenic system, enabling it to lock onto less intense heat sources, such as the hot CO_2 gas in the target's exhaust plume, visible from anywhere around the aircraft. Careful design of the proximity fuze ensures that although the missile is aiming at the plume, its warhead will be detonated as close to the aircraft as possible. The AIM-9L is called an "all-aspect" missile because, unlike earlier versions, it will lock onto a target from any angle.

Now under development is the latest version of the Sidewinder, the AIM-9R, with an imaging IR (IIR) seeker. In place of a single detector, the IIR seeker has an array of hundreds of miniature detectors which can assemble a detailed image of the target. IIR seekers have been used for air-to-surface weapons, such as the AGM-65D Maverick, for some time, and have now been miniaturized to the point where they will fit in an AAM. The advantage of IIR seekers is that they respond to a target's size as well as to its heat intensity, and will therefore lock onto cooler targets, or lower-contrast targets, that other seekers will not track reliably. The AIM-9R should be even more accurate than the AIM-9L, and much less likely to be duped by countermeasures such as flares.

The absorption of IR radiation in the atmosphere tends to limit the range of IR missiles to ten to fifteen miles, and Sidewinder has proven reliable, so ASRAAM has little chance of achieving significant advances in those areas. It will, however, introduce some more major improvements. Like AMRAAM, but unlike the AIM-9L, it will be a tail-controlled missile for greater maneuverability, and will be more lethal against highly agile targets, and targets at close range. Smaller and lighter than the AIM-9, it will have an IIR seeker, but like AMRAAM it will also have an inertial

British Aerospace produced Sky Flash, basically a new missile packed into the AIM-7 airframe, in the mid-1970s. An improved version with active-radar homing, designated Rb71a, is to form the main armament of Sweden's Gripen fighter. (British Aerospace)

reference unit for dead-reckoning navigation, and a standard computer interface so that it can be initialized before launch.

In the case of the short-range missile, this will mean that it can be used against a target detected by radar, even in the presence of clouds; the missile can be directed toward the target under the control of its inertial unit, and will detect it autonomously when it emerges from the cloud. Also, the combination of a helmet-mounted display and the inertially-guided function will permit the pilot to designate a target which is well off the boresight of the aircraft. The pilot's head angle as he holds the HMD sighting symbol on the target will be translated into a hearing and elevation, and programmed into the ASRAAM before launch. After launch, once again, the missile will fly under inertial control until its seeker picks up the target.

Other types of missiles are being considered for development, but will not see service until the late 1990s. The US Navy, for instance, is working on its Advanced AAM (AAAM), a Sparrow-sized weapon in the 100-mile-range class to succeed the very large and expensive Phoenix. Using the AAAM will allow the F-14 to patrol further from the carrier group, increasing its chances of intercepting Backfire bombers

The AIM-132 ASRAAM (advanced short-range air-to-air missile) is the intended successor to the AIM-9. It is smaller and more agile than the AIM-9 and will have an advanced focal-plane-array homing head. The system includes a compact high-pressure air generator built into the pylon, so that the missile can remain active and seek targets throughout a combat. (British Aerospace)

before they can launch missiles at the fleet. It may be the first air-to-air missile to use ramjet propulsion to extend its range.

The air-to-air antiradiation missile (AA-ARM) is something that has been discussed and studied (one such weapon, the Hughes Brazo, was investigated in the early 1970s) but not, as far as is known, developed for operational use. However, it is such a logical extension of known technology that it would not be surprising if it had been tested, or even fielded, under a "black" or secret program. As its name suggests, the AA-ARM would home in on the radar signals from a hostile aircraft, possibly switching to an IR mode in the terminal stage. Radio-frequency or microwave emissions can be intercepted accurately at very long range, because the signals have not been scattered, like a normal radar reflection, and have to travel only one way. The AA-ARM could be initialized before launch with the help of the fighter's own passive detection systems.

More conventional technology can also be applied in different ways. While NATO is planning to use AMRAAM and ASRAAM, France is developing a single missile to cover both requirements, the Matra MICA (Missile d'Interception et de Combat Aerien). Using more advanced electronic technology than was available when AMRAAM was designed, MICA is intended to fall about halfway between AMRAAM and ASRAAM in size, and will be produced in active-radar and IR versions, both with inertial guidance.

At one point, the USAF's ATF program office let it be known that it was considering whether the new fighter should have a gun, or whether the effectiveness of new AAMs was such that the gun was no longer necessary. The howl of protest from the pilot community soon put a stop to that line of thinking, and—as far as present plans are concerned—the ATF will have a gun, like all other fighters known to be under development.

There are three basic types of fighter gun in service, all derived from designs developed between 1940 and 1946, when increasing speeds in air combat were putting excessive demands on the average pilot's marksmanship. A higher rate of fire than was possible with conventional machine guns or cannons was deemed desirable to compensate for aiming errors. German designers developed two high-rate-of-fire weapons: a twin-barrel gun with mechanically linked barrels, known as the GAST, and the Mauser MG 213 revolver cannon, which combined belt feed with revolver-type multiple chambers. The MG 213 never entered service, but was enthusiastically copied by all the victorious Allies as the British Aden, the French DEFA, the American Pontiac M-39 and various Soviet weapons. Somewhat later, in the mid-1960s, the Soviet Union adopted the GAST principle for the GSh-23 cannon, which is fitted to the later marks of MiG-21 and the MiG-23.

The heaviest, most complex and most lethal gun, however, was that developed by the USAF and General Electric under Project Vulcan, which started in 1946. Based on the original machine gun, developed by Dr. Richard Gatling during the Civil War, this weapon had six barrels revolving around a common axis, each at a different point in its firing cycle. It took a long time to be adopted and was not really successful until it was mated with a fully powered feed system, in the F-105. In Vietnam, it was used in the F-105 and A-7D, in pods under early-model F-4s, and in the nose of the USAF's F-4E.

The argument between advocates of the revolver cannon and the Gatling's supporters continues to this day. The revolver cannon is lighter, and although it has a

This F-4G is a Wild Weasel, fitted with a sophisticated system to detect hostile radars and determine their position, and armed with anti-radiation missiles (ARMs) which home on to such radars. Future fighters may carry air-to-air ARMs. (McDonnell Douglas)

much lower rate of fire—1,700 rounds per minute, versus 6,000 for the Gatling—it reaches its maximum rate more quickly and thus fires almost as many shots in the first vital half-second after the firing button is depressed. Advocates of the Gatling and its powered feed system note that both are more reliable than revolver cannon and normal linked belt feeds. If a round does not fire, it does not stop the operation of the gun, which is powered by hydraulic motors. The feed system, a high-speed conveyor which is also externally powered, handles each round individually, so that there are no links to break under the stress of high firing rates.

The Eurofighter EFA will have a single revolver cannon, like the JAS 39 and Lavi; the ATF will almost certainly have a Gatling. Under a program called Advanced Gun Technology (AGT), the USAF has studied new guns using "case-telescoped" ammunition (sometimes called the "beer-can round") in which most of the propellant is formed into a cylinder around the projectile with a small amount at its base. The charge burns from the base upward, so that the flame front remains behind the shell as it leaves the case. Case-telescoped rounds can attain very high muzzle velocity, improving accuracy and lethality, and because of their plain cylindrical shape they can be stored and handled very efficiently.

The most serious competition for such a weapon, however, is the veteran M61, in an improved version now under development. This would have nineteen-inch-longer barrels than the current weapon, and would fire improved ammunition with more powerful propellant, a pyrotechnic fuze and a lighter, more aerodynamic projectile. The weapon's muzzle velocity would be increased from 3,380 feet per second to more than 3,900 feet per second. The barrels would be wrapped in composite material to reduce their weight, and the ammunition cases would be aluminum, rather than brass. Together with other material changes, this would reduce the weight of a complete system—gun, feed system and ammunition—from 795 pounds to 605 pounds. Perhaps its most attractive feature, though, would be its low development costs compared with a new gun.

Even so, 605 pounds is a great deal of weight in fighter terms, and is almost as much as a pair of AMRAAMs. Even a single revolver cannon like the Mauser BK 27 or the Aden 25 weighs 430-450 pounds, including ammunition. The weight and drag of the extra airframe volume needed to carry the weapon must also be considered, so the penalty is even greater than the weight of the gun and ammunition alone. Say, for example, that the total penalty of putting a single gun on the EFA is about 600 pounds. If the gun was to be eliminated, the Eurofighter designers could replace the new EJ200 engine with an uprated version of the F404, achieve the same flight performance and save about half a billion dollars in engine development costs.

The problem is that, while computer studies consistently show that the gun is not worth its weight, computer studies have consistently shown the same result since the first AAMs were developed and, in actual combat, the computer studies have consistently been proven to be wrong. In practice, the combination of the long-range missile, the short-range missile and the gun builds "graceful degradation" into the fighter weapon system. If the long-range missile fails or is countered, the short-range missile can be used as the range closes to ten to twelve miles; if the short-range

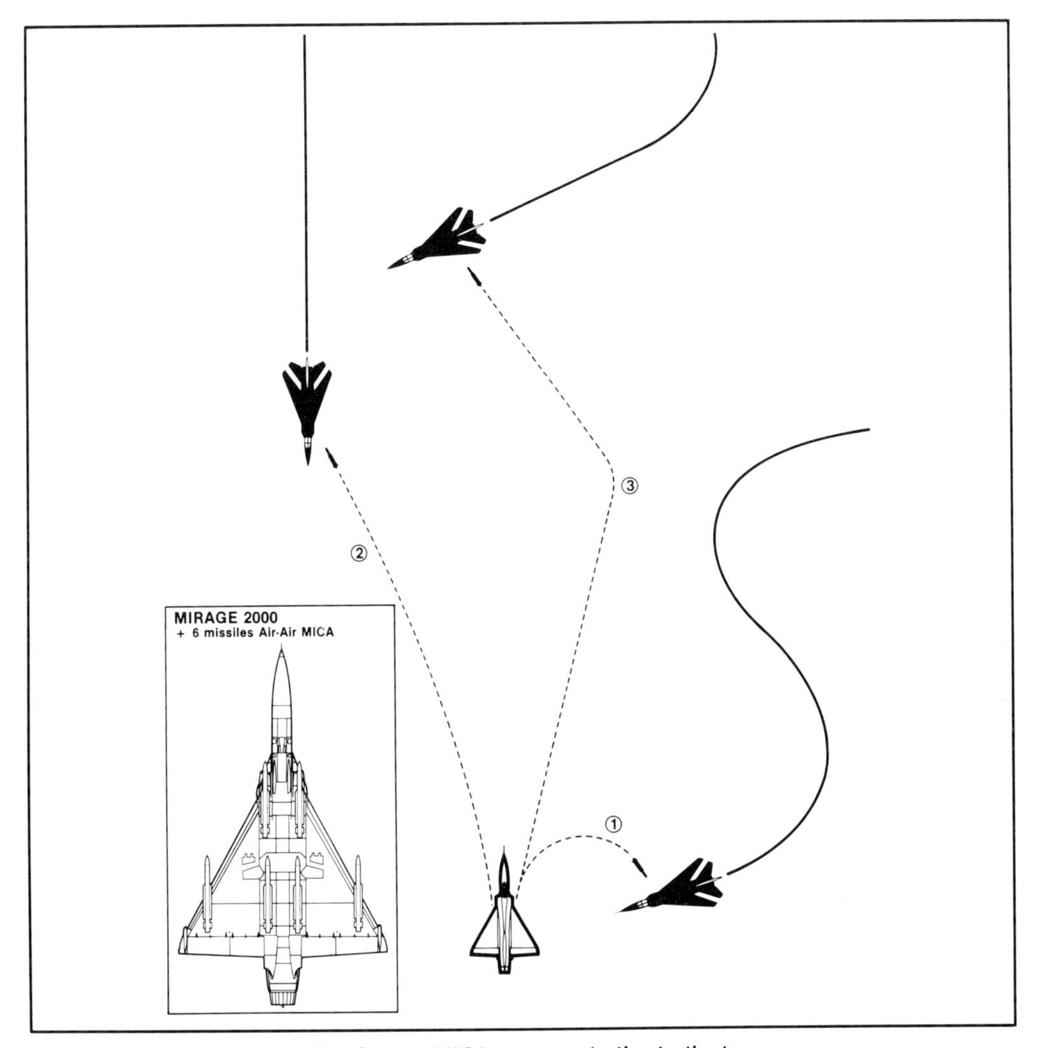

France's Matra company is developing MICA, a new missile similar in concept to AMRAAM but designed to be smaller and cheaper than the US missile, with a shorter maximum range. A fighter such as the Mirage 2000 (inset) could carry six MICA missiles. The operational modes illustrated here are the same as those of AMRAAM. In example 1, the missile is initialized with the predicted position of the target, navigates toward that point under inertial guidance, and acquires the target with its active homing head. In example 2, the missile's radar acquires the target while it is still on the wing, and it pulls an extremely tight turn, using thrust vectoring, to engage it. In the third example, at maximum range, the launch aircraft updates the missile in mid-flight to take account of the target's maneuvers. (GIFAS)

missile is unsuccessful, or the pilot simply runs out of weapons, the gun is available. There is also no frustration like that of the fighter pilot who sees a "sitter" cross in front of him 500 yards away, but cannot engage it because the safety features of the missile fuze will not let it arm itself in time. One basic advantage of the gun is that it is, as General Electric puts it, "irrefutable": once the attacker achieves a firing solution and fires, there is absolutely no evasive maneuver or countermeasure available.

Ways of improving aerial gunnery are still being developed and, just like the rapid-firing cannon and the original gyroscopic and radar gunsights, they reflect the sensible recognition that not all good pilots will ever be good shots. General Electric, for example, has developed Aim-Guns, a computer model that can be adapted to fit almost any aircraft with a digital head-up display. Aim-Guns generates a pair of curved lines on the HUD, resembling a drawing of a funnel cloud, which give a rough indication of ballistic drop over range: in straight-and-level flight, for example, an average fighter-sized target is in the path of the shots when its wings touch the sides of the funnel. As the attacker maneuvers to track the target, the funnel curves because the track of the shells falls away from that of the aircraft. In any event, the attacking pilot's job is to steer the funnel over the target. General Electric claims a considerable improvement in accuracy, particularly under difficult circumstances where average shooters have trouble: angles of forty to sixty degrees off the tail, ranges of more than 1,000 feet, and situations in which the radar is jammed.

The all-new ATF may well use a more sophisticated method of aiming guns, known as integrated flight and fire control (IFFC). This was spectacularly demonstrated in August 1982, when an outwardly unmodified F-15 Eagle engaged a PQM-102 high-performance drone over the New Mexico desert. The drone was pulling a 4 g turn at high subsonic speed, and the F-15 pilot opened fire from a point fifty degrees off the target's nose, at a range of 5,800 feet. Just under two seconds later, the pilot ceased firing, 3,800 feet from the target. Normally, such a shot would be considered next to impossible. As far as could be discerned from the wreckage, however, thirty out of the 171 shots hit the PQM-102, rupturing its fuel tanks and destroying its engine even though the shells were inert.

No changes to the gun or airframe had been made to permit this superhuman feat of marksmanship. The only modifications to the F-15 were electronic, and provided a means for its APG-63 radar, its flight control system and its HUD to work together. The IFFC system displayed a box on the HUD, and the pilot needed only to put the sight reticle and the target within the box. The system then automatically steered the aircraft in pitch, roll and yaw, up to its physical limits, to cancel out ballistic and lead factors, and gave the pilot a firing cue. Such a system should be relatively easy to implement on ATF, with its advanced avionics.

With AMRAAM, ASRAAM and highly accurate guns, the fighters of the 1990s will wield an overlapping spectrum of weapons capable of engaging targets from point-blank range to sixty miles. How well these are used, however, and how the air battle is fought, will be a matter of tactics, training and, ultimately, the skill of one pilot matched against another.

Chapter 7

Air combat in the 1990s

"The fighter pilots should have an allotted area to cruise around in as it suits them, but when they see an opponent they must attack and shoot him down. Anything else is absurd." Manfred von Richthofen's words of 1917 are still nailed up above the bar in more than a few fighter bases. They may never have constituted a complete doctrine of air combat, but they have weathered the test of time in much better shape than any number of war-college studies.

The history of air combat has fallen into cycles of theory and practice. Generally, practical experience has demolished the previously accepted theories and, immediately after the conflict, has led to the development of new doctrines. Unfortunately, conflict has often driven forward the evolution and application of new technologies; maturing in peacetime, they seem to render the lessons of the past war obsolete. What was learned in Korea, for example, was forgotten as supersonic fighters, with powerful radar systems and long-range air-to-air missiles (AAMs), began to enter service, and it was only Vietnam that revealed the limitations of these so-called flying Cadillacs. Most current fighters are part of the post-Vietnam cycle, combining the merits of the traditional visual fighter—visibility, relaxed handling limits and good ergonomics—with supersonic speed and a much expanded maneuver envelope. Combat experience also spurred another major technological advance, in the shape of reliable, increased-aspect short-range AAMs.

Battles over the Falklands and the Beka'a Valley have shown that the new technology works as predicted. The Falklands provided a particularly interesting case, in that the Sea Harrier, the only fighter on the winning side, was not a high-g fighter, and would not generally have been considered in the same class as its supersonic adversaries. But the armament, ergonomics and cockpit visibility of the Sea Harrier were up to new-generation standards, and probably accounted in part for the type's effectiveness in combat.

However, extreme danger lies in assuming once again, on the basis of limited operational experience, that current hardware and doctrine have solved all the problems of air warfare. As the 1990s draw closer, the unresolved issues will become more important.

Perhaps the most important issue facing fighter commanders as they look to the 1990s is the sheer density of the air battle. When one engagement may involve dozens of fighters on either side, as was the case over Lebanon in 1982, the problem

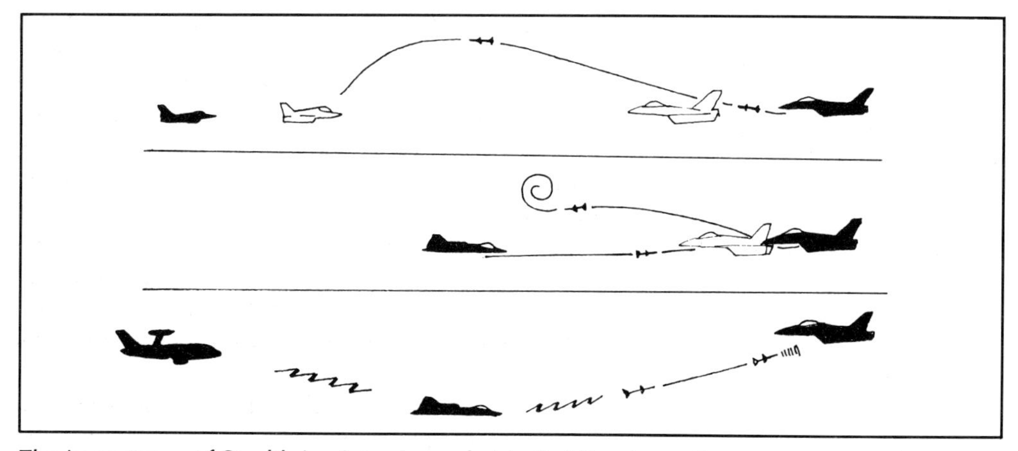

The importance of Stealth in air-to-air combat is that it reduces the adversary's detection range, reduces the range at which an active or semi-active missile can lock on, and reduces the F-pole, or the distance between the launch aircraft and the target at impact. In the engagement depicted at the top, the aircraft at right has a more powerful radar and longer-range missiles than the aircraft on the left, and takes the first shot. Center, a low-observable fighter, left, may reach launching parameters with an IR missile before the fighter with a semi-active weapon can complete the engagement. Bottom, the Stealth fighter at left receives target range and position information from an AEW&C aircraft and transmits it to an AMRAAM-type weapon; the target has no idea he is under attack until the missile's active seeker locks on.

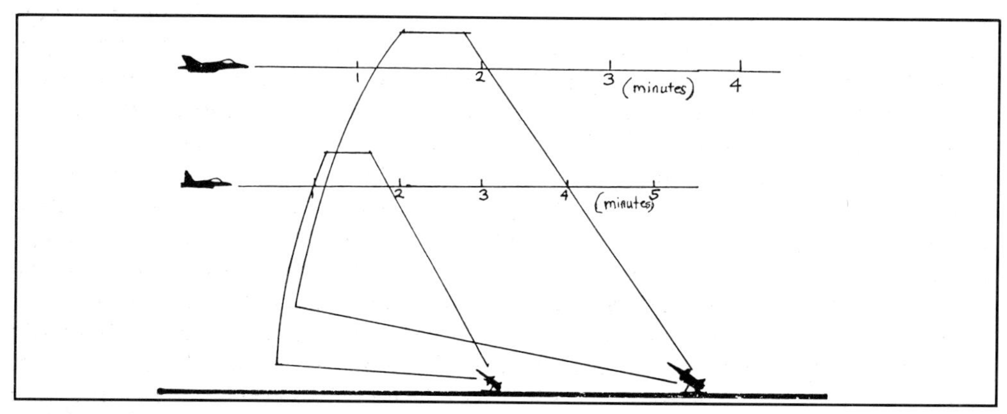

Height and speed are effective counters to the SAM threat. A supersonic-cruise, high-altitude fighter here traverses the lethal envelope of a medium-range SAM in about one minute; a subsonic fighter, at a lower altitude, is at risk three times longer, and at one point faces a dual threat as it passes within lethal range of a smaller, mobile weapon.

is that any realistic system of battle management breaks down during a few minutes of intense combat. With dozens of targets and threats spread over hundreds of square miles horizontally and four to five miles vertically, launch-and-leave missiles with ranges above ten miles, and no reliable means of telling friend from enemy beyond visual range, formation tactics are likely to give way to individual combat. Even if the odds in any one combat are favorable, the probability of defeat rapidly increases in a sequence of single contests.

The remarkable effectiveness of all-aspect IR missiles has changed close combat since the Vietnam era. Older missiles required the pilot to maneuver into a "lethal cone" defined by a narrow angle off the target's tail, forcing most dogfights into turning engagements. This is no longer the case, and it has important implications in offense and defense.

Optimizing the use of all-aspect weapons currently depends on the ability to point the nose of the aircraft rapidly toward the target, placing it within the missile's lethal envelope. "Nose authority," as this is called, means not only the ability to sustain high g, but the ability to generate even higher turn rates very quickly. The F-18 represents the state of the art in close combat, with a combination of advanced aerodynamics (maneuvering flaps and large leading-edge root extensions), good engine handling and an excellent flight-control system, which makes it possible to exploit the aircraft's characteristics to the fullest degree. The new canards will be even more energetic, because of their ability to generate very high turning moments, to move the heavy fuselage around its axis, while retaining their full net lift. ATF will couple such advanced aerodynamics with the mission-adaptive wing, vectored thrust and highly integrated, automated control of the aircraft and engine.

The use of thrust vectoring in combat is controversial, however. Advocates of so-called supermaneuverable fighters, using thrust vectoring and advanced aerodynamic design to remain fully controllable well beyond the normal aerodynamic stall, argue that they will be able to engage targets over a much larger area than conventional fighters. Opponents argue that aggressive post-stall maneuvers and vectored or reversing thrust kill the fighter's energy much more rapidly than conventional maneuvering, and leave it vulnerable to a second attacker. One counterargument is that a supermaneuverable fighter's ability to virtually pivot on its axis would allow it to evade a less agile attacker and re-engage it from a more favorable aspect in a single maneuver, while other members of the hostile formation would be effectively excluded from the fight for as long as it took them to complete their own turns.

The ability to sustain a high-g turn is now taken for granted, and is still a basic parameter of fighter performance. Because of the all-aspect missile threat, however, almost any sustained maneuver is a risky procedure in close combat, no matter how fast or how tight it might be. Quicker entry to and exit from maneuvers, and a fanatical avoidance of straight-line flight will be the keys to survival.

In the last few years an unexpected limit to combat maneuverability has been discovered, not in aerodynamics or in thrust/weight ratio but in human physiology: a phenomenon called g-induced loss of consciousness (G-LOC).

G-LOC is not the same as "blacking out," in which blood drains from the pilot's head and his vision first contracts to a tunnel and disappears. G-LOC is much more dangerous, and can occur when a pilot is subjected to a rapid increase in g to a high level (above 5 g) or when sustained high g-loads are followed by a further increase. Under such circumstances, the body's normal defense mechanisms–such as increased heart rate and blood pressure–do not work rapidly or effectively enough to maintain blood pressure in the brain. If this drops below a critical level, the pilot loses consciousness suddenly and completely.

A pilot will recover from a blackout as soon as the g-loading is relaxed, but this is not the case with G-LOC. The pilot will be out cold for ten to thirty seconds–fifteen seconds is the average, and even after he comes to, there is a phase during which he is conscious but unresponsive. "The lights are on but nobody is home," says a USAF researcher. "You can hear your wingman screaming at you, but it doesn't mean anything." This stage is probably connected with the re-oxygenation of the brain tissue. A complete G-LOC episode can easily leave the pilot out of control and unable to eject for forty-five seconds or more, long enough to crash even from a relatively high altitude.

Fighters of the F-4 generation could not generate g fast enough to enter the G-LOC regime, but the problem emerged with the introduction of aircraft such as the F-16, which is not only physically capable of generating rapid increases in g, but also has a high-authority g-limiting function in its flight control system. "The way the young pilots of today fly the F-16 is to give it the maximum control input and let the system handle the overshoot," says one experienced USAF pilot. On other aircraft, a similar input would probably result in the aircraft exceeding its g limit. The ATF and other new fighters will emulate the F-16's characteristics in this respect.

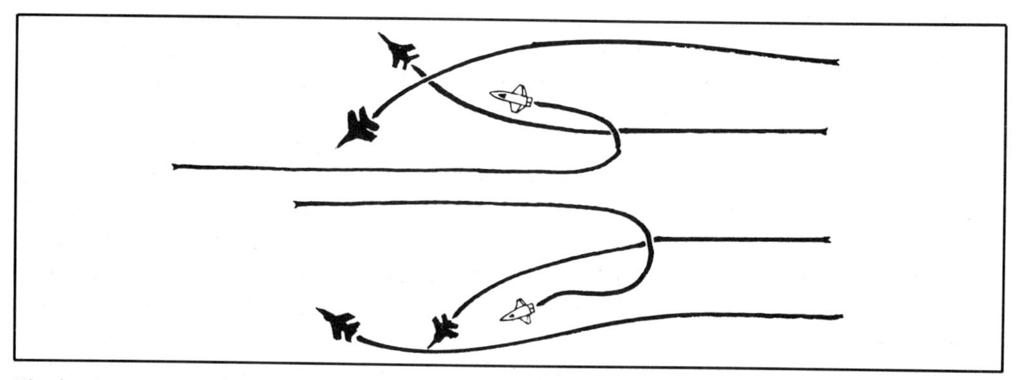

The basic argument for supermaneuverability (the ability to turn at low airspeed and high g, within a very small radius) is that an aircraft which cannot emulate such a maneuver can be prevented from bringing its weapons to bear. Here, after an initially inconclusive head-on engagement, two super-agile fighters have inverted the odds against four more cumbersome hostiles.

The danger of G-LOC was brought home in tragic fashion to the world of military aviation when two of the three prototypes of Northrop's F-20 Tigershark fighter crashed during demonstration routines, killing their pilots, only months apart. (One was lost during a demonstration at Suwon, South Korea, in October 1984, and the other crashed at Goose Bay, Newfoundland, in May 1985, during practice for the Paris Air Show.) While G-LOC had probably caused several earlier F-16 accidents – one of its most dangerous attributes is that it leaves no physical traces – both the Suwon and Goose accidents and the flying sequences before them had been carefully filmed, pointed to this recently identified phenomenon as the cause of the accidents.

Researchers are working on improvements to the G-suit, highly reclined seats and other physiological approaches to the G-LOC problem, but the best that can be hoped for is that it will be alleviated, and that the envelope within which it is likely to occur may be reduced. The other avenue of approach is to develop a system that constantly monitors whether the pilot is conscious (something that sounds simpler than it is). Without planting electrodes in the pilot's head, which is considered unacceptable, there are no reliable and unambiguous indicators of consciousness than can be remotely monitored. Now under study by the US Air Force is something called LOCOMS (loss of consciousness monitoring system), described as "a jury" of sensors.

There are a number of attributes that could be sensed by LOCOMS. Is the pilot's head erect and moving? Does he have a grip on the throttle and stick, and how strong is it? Is there any seizure activity? Is he performing a straining movement to resist g, and how strongly, measured by pulsations in the oxygen mask? What is his blood pressure at eye level? What is his blink rate? (The last parameter can be measured by a small electro-optical sensor attached to the oxygen mask.)

Also under development for the LOCOMS program is a miniature radar device which can monitor the pulse in the superficial temporal artery. An outside contender, but a potentially very effective sensor, is a magnetoencephalograph (MEG), a device that responds to the magnetic element of the electric fields inside the brain. If an MEG detects large, slow "delta waves" in the brain, the pilot is almost certainly unconscious. The problem is developing an MEG that will fit in the helmet; not an impossibility but a major engineering challenge.

The sensors will be linked to the aircraft databus, to give them a g history of the aircraft. An expert system will be used to evaluate the sensor outputs continuously and determine whether the pilot is conscious or not. If the system diagnoses G-LOC, a synthesized voice will ask the pilot whether he is awake and give him a chance to override the system. If the pilot does not respond, LOCOMS will instruct the aircraft's flight management system to follow a safe flight path until the pilot indicates he is ready to resume control.

Primarily, though, such a system will be useful during training, and to avoid peacetime accidents. Even if the aircraft is equipped to save itself and the pilot after a G-LOC, it will be highly vulnerable to attack while the pilot recovers, and its pilot will be performing poorly after he comes to.

Therefore, tactics and training will have to be designed to avoid the G-LOC zone. Future tactics may stress a "turn-shoot-go" approach, combining rapid short-duration maneuvers with quick acceleration, avoiding G-LOC and making the best use of missiles while presenting a very difficult, unpredictable target to an adversary.

Some of the new technology in ATF and other fighters will improve the pilot's chances in a short-range engagement. As noted above, modern short-range missiles have a very large lethal envelope. The problem is that the missile's lethal envelope is not a neat cone, but a set of parameters influenced by a target's range, bearing, track and speed, and the rates of change of all these. Also, it may be excessively limiting to fire only when the probability of a kill is 100 percent; if another member of his formation is threatened, for example, a pilot may fire a missile with a much lower kill probability if it will force the hostile to break off his attack. At the edge of the envelope, particularly in off-boresight engagements, these parameters become more critical, but it is precisely at that point where current aircraft have no way of computing the odds of a successful shot and relaying that information to the pilot.

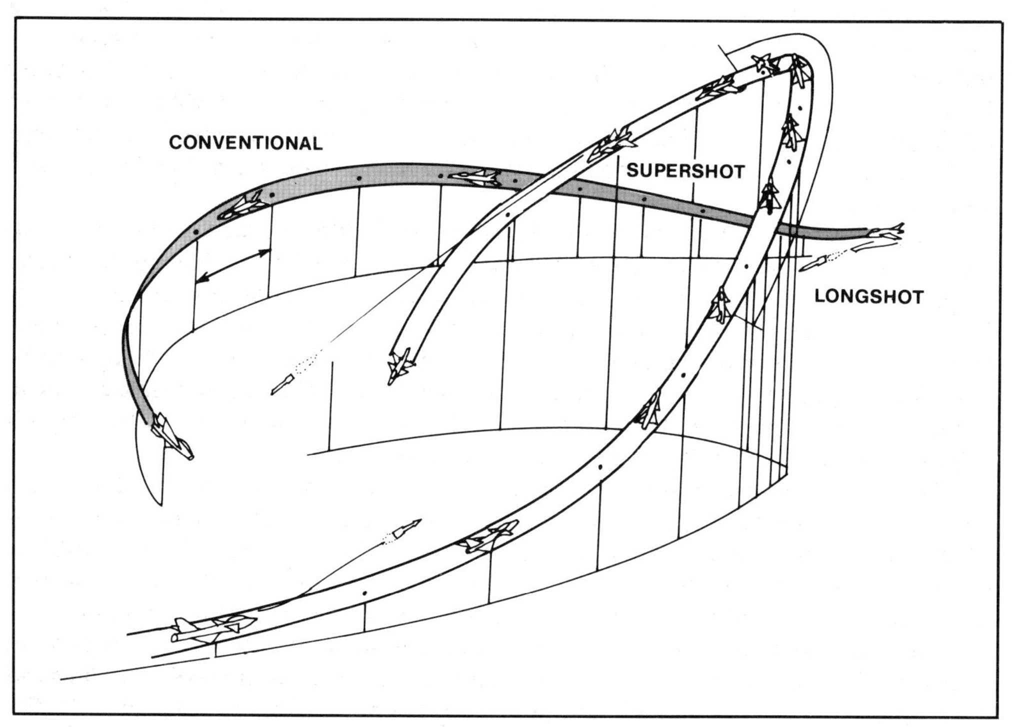

A supermaneuverable aircraft, approaching from the left, may be able to pull the type of maneuver seen in the top right-hand corner in order to re-engage an enemy from an advantageous aspect. A conventional aircraft would be unable to trade speed for height as quickly as the post-stalled superagile fighter, and would be unable to cope with the combination of low speed and drastic sideslip angles needed for the topple at the apex of the turn.

The helmet-mounted display (HMD) will be the key to developing successful tactics, enabling the pilot to keep his head over the side while communicating aircraft and missile information to the pilot. Simulations have already shown that the use of an HMD, together with missile seekers slaved to the pilot's head movements and a control system programmed with missile parameters, will make it possible to achieve a more lethal missile launch solution in less time. In one case, the pilot with an HMD could fire eight seconds earlier than the pilot aiming through the HUD. He could reach firing solutions more often, and more of the missiles that were fired found their targets.

While technology is making it a great deal easier to hit the enemy, it is a corollary that close combat will become a great deal more dangerous, because a lethal threat can now appear from almost any direction. In a world of all-aspect, off-boresight weapons, "watching your six" will no longer be enough. As a result, in an intense air battle, the number of hostiles in a position to pose a threat within a few seconds will greatly increase.

Some new-technology features will help in the defensive fight. For example, a new fighter could be equipped with a dual-mode warning system, combining a millimeter-wave radar with an infrared sensor, which would scan the sky all around the aircraft for signs of a missile launch. The Pilot Associate system will provide more intelligent management of countermeasures, including jamming and the automated ejection of chaff and flares, helping to counter the reduced gullibility of new-generation missiles.

Thrust reversal and vectoring are also likely to be effective means of evasion. Attacked with an IR missile, an ATF pilot applies full reverse thrust while automatically dispensing flares. The aircraft decelerates, but the decoys do not slow down as rapidly, moving out ahead of the aircraft. Meanwhile, the fighter's real exhaust plume is split into top and bottom vertical components, where it is very quickly dissipated by colliding at right angles with the ambient air. Faced with a choice between a drastically reduced real signature at a changed velocity, and a strong decoy on the target's original course, the missile is very likely to be deceived.

Another advantage of thrust reversal is that it permits an aircraft to slow down without any visual cues such as the extension of an airbrake or a change in pitch attitude. An attacking pilot will not be able to respond to a speed reduction until he detects that the rate of closure between his aircraft and the target has diminished, and may be forced into an evasive maneuver to avoid overshooting the target.

Statistics and simulations, however, continue to show that sixty to ninety percent of pilots who are shot down never see their attacker. Even with HMS and all-round warning systems, survival in a long-duration "furball" could be a matter of luck. The risk of taking losses due to pilot saturation and the whims of fate is unacceptable to any commander. Losing a $35 million fighter, including its $14 million avionics system, to a novice pilot in a $5 million MiG-21 is nobody's idea of an exchange rate.

At this point, a popular myth concerning fighter pilots has to be dispelled. Fighter pilots are not the modern descendants of the medieval knights of romantic fiction, living for the thrill of a one-to-one joust with the enemy. Successful fighter pilots want to destroy the enemy and *survive*. Surprise and deception are tools of the trade. So is "initiative control," or the fighter leader's ability to give or decline combat according to whether the circumstances are favorable. If you have a choice, it is neither brave nor honorable to enter an engagement against superior odds, with the tactical situation against you: the word is *dumb*. When the circumstances point the other way, and the enemy's strength is locally inferior and his position less advantageous, you stand a good chance of destroying a number of aircraft and, by disrupting the formation, force the others to withdraw. (Forcing an enemy to abandon his mission is, rightly, termed a "mission kill.") But if the game is loaded against you, as in the case of close combat with a superior number of inferior aircraft, don't play.

The alternative to a thirty-fighter furball is to place more emphasis on diminishing the enemy's strength before such a battle. One way of doing this is to attack smaller tactical formations at long range before they can be assembled into bewildering armadas over the battlefield. Another approach is to attack airborne systems such as AEW&C aircraft, intelligence-gathering aircraft and stand-off jammers, all of which multiply the effectiveness of the hostile force as long as they are operational.

The most physically obvious of the means by which ATF is intended to reach and destroy these targets are supersonic cruise and Stealth. The use of high speed and high altitude to evade SAMs was part of the ATF philosophy at a very early stage. However, the ATF's ability to operate at supersonic speed for more than a few minutes in each mission, and to maneuver at supersonic speed, will give it a considerable advantage in fighter-versus-fighter actions.

A Northrop paper published in 1981 provided a very simple analogy between fighters roaming the rear of the battle area and cue balls coasting around a pool table. If one ball is moving much faster than the others, a fairly simple analysis shows that it will close on the tracks of slower balls from the rear much more often than the slower balls will close on its track. The analogy shows that, other things being equal,

Ultimately, the factor which will decide most future air battles is the training, experience and prowess of the pilot at the stick of the fastest and most complex of weapons.

the faster fighter will tend to approach its opponents from the rear, out of sight of their radars, and may often have the advantage of surprise.

Speed and height, too, can give the ATF the advantage in terms of initiative control. Conventional subsonic-cruise fighters may still be able to force an engagement, but only at the expense of using their afterburners. Even so, the ATFs may be able to maneuver to avoid them at supersonic speed without using full augmented power, and resume their mission.

Stealth opens up a completely new aspect of air combat. Col. Albert C. Piccirillo, director of the ATF program office up to the end of 1986, has compared the new fighter's use of Stealth to the emergence of the U-boat in the 1914–18 war. The objective is "to kill without being seen, disengage and disappear," he said in late 1985. "The last thing you do is surface and use the deck gun . . . close-in combat is something you try to avoid." The idea is to use Stealth to provide the ATF pilot with the advantage of the first look, seeing the target before its pilot can see him. Stealth does not make ATF invisible, though. Eventually, either the target's own radar will detect the ATF, or a third radar on the ground or in an AEW&C aircraft will see it and direct the target's attention toward it. The goal of ATF tactics, therefore, is to make the best possible use of the first stage of an engagement, the valuable minutes or seconds during which the target is unaware of the attacker's presence.

This is where the battle-management functions provided by the Pilot's Associate systems could play a decisive role. Even before takeoff, sitting in the cockpit inside a hardened shelter, the ATF pilot could call up his mission plan on the cockpit displays, and update it according to the latest JTIDS data. The location of SAM systems and the most probable target tracks could all be revised and rehearsed before the mission.

Once in flight, at the touch of a switch or by voice command, the pilot could transform one of the wide-screen displays into a "God's-eye-view" of the developing engagement, clearly showing the positions of the target, SAM systems and other aircraft in the area. Given that the target may be more than 100 miles away at the start of the engagement, there are likely to be many of these in some position to influence the battle.

Through the interactive display, the pilot can not only look at what other systems are operating in the area, but also at their performance relative to his aircraft. The system may, for example, be able to tell him that if he passes within twenty miles of an SA-11 radar, there is a twenty-five percent chance that he will be detected. He may take that chance in order to optimize his approach to the target.

The leader of the ATF formation can use the PA system to gather information on the other aircraft, or to designate individual targets for the rest of the group. Interconnecting PA systems also allow the leader to know how much fuel and armament remain on board the other aircraft in the formation.

As the targets approach the maximum launch range of the ATF's AMRAAM missiles, the pilot will plan his attack. At this point, the value of remaining undetected has to be balanced against the importance of an effective missile shot. The pilot may decide that attack is the priority, and will go to full augmented thrust, surging toward Mach 2.5 and 70,000 feet with three times the acceleration of an F-15. At the same time, the phased-array radar will enter its raid-assessment mode, closely scanning the hostile formation and assigning an individual track to each target.

Alternatively, the pilot may feel confident, perhaps on the basis of JTIDS or other data, that he knows the strength of the formation. He may continue to cruise at Mach 1.4, without leaving an unambiguous trace on the hostiles' infrared search and track displays, and with his radar generating just enough power to break out the individual targets from the cluster and automatically varying its signals to reduce the probability that they will be intercepted. Offering his minimal nose-on radar image to the hostiles' radars, he remains undetected. Even the firing of the first two AMRAAMs, virtually smokeless and without the telltale electronic signature of a semi-active missile's illuminating beam, is invisible at thirty miles range. The ATF pilot's next action, remarkably, is to slow down with reverse thrust, slowing the rate of closure and increasing the F-pole. As his PA system informs him that the missiles are autonomous, he breaks sharply, reaccelerates and begins a long, supersonic turn around the hostile formation's flank.

The hostiles' first indication that they are under attack is when the first AMRAAM blows the tail off the leader's aircraft. The second weapon explodes close enough to another aircraft to damage its fuel tanks and force it to head for the nearest runway. The remaining two aircraft, uncertain as to how many aircraft have engaged them, sensibly elect to withdraw and fight another day. This is the "bolt from the blue" attack; Sir Galahad might not approve, but the Red Baron most certainly would.

Index